TRINITY
BATMAN • SUPERMAN • WONDER WOMAN

BATMAN
SUPERMAN
WONDER WOMAN

MATT WAGNER WRITER/ARTIST

COLLECTION COVER BY MATT WAGNER WITH BRENNAN

SUPERMAN CREATED BY JERRY SIEGEL AND JOE SHUSTER

WONDER WOMAN CREATED BY

DAVE STEWART COLORIST SEAN KONOT LETTERER

WAGNER BATMAN CREATED BY BOB KANE WITH BILL FINGER

BY SPECIAL ARRANGEMENT WITH THE JERRY SIEGEL FAMILY

WILLIAM MOULTON MARSTON

BATMAN/SUPERMAN/WONDER WOMAN: TRINITY

DC Comics, 2900 West Alameda Ave., Burbank, CA 91505
Printed by LSC Communications, Owensville, MO, USA. 6/23/17. First Printing.
ISBN: 978-1-4012-7127-5

Library of Congress Cataloging-in-Publication Data is available.

Introduction by **Brad Meltzer**

The icons are the hardest. It's true. Superman. Batman. Wonder Woman. All icons. All difficult. But it's not because the characters themselves are impossible to define. Actually, it's the opposite. Superman, Batman and Wonder Woman are perfectly defined. Honed over 60 years by some of the world's finest writers and artists, the trinity of heroes is so well developed that their actions and reactions can almost be predicted. And that's the hard part.

Like writing the final season of *Cheers* or *M*A*S*H* or *Seinfeld*, how do you add anything original to the pantheon when everything's already been done? The answer is not easy, but at least you have the characters. It's the one advantage of writing the icons. Even the most mundane story is suddenly dressed up when you add Superman, Batman and Wonder Woman. But like writing those last seasons of *Cheers*, *M*A*S*H* or *Seinfeld*, adding Cliff & Norm, BJ & Hawkeye, or Jerry & George only gets you good.

It's easy to do good. Anyone can do good. What's hard is something great.

TRINITY is great. And not just great as in the slightly more complimentary version of good. In these forthcoming pages, Matt Wagner digs through the psyches of the icons and unearths true greatness. Make no mistake: this is not a simple superhero story. Wagner starts with Superman, Batman and Wonder Woman—but he explores Clark, Bruce and Diana.

It's in that humanity that TRINITY finds something new—and in that new, makes us feel the excitement of meeting these characters for the first time—even as they meet each other. We've been married to these characters for years—knowing everything about them... every last detail. But as the years pile on, as the special settles into the mundane, we start questioning whether the old flame will ever be rekindled. And then...when we least expect it, the moonlight hits them just right, a memory door opens and all the original emotions flood right back. And that is magic.

Like a master magician, forcing us to focus on the decoy of his moving hand, Wagner waves the capes and cowls to get our attention. But what causes our mouths to gape open is the simplicity of what's hidden underneath—the magical moments of humanity that have always been there, somehow previously unseen.

Superman is not new. Batman is not new. Wonder Woman is not new. Yet, Wagner still finds vital details no one's ever thought of before: From the idea that super-hearing is the hardest power to resist...to the simple concept that while the trains in Metropolis run on time, Clark misses one at least three times a week to keep up appearances. From Bruce's surprise that Clark can find him so quickly...to Clark's internal admission that Bruce is hard to miss with a beltful of tracking devices...to Bizarro's simple-minded "Racer Cool" for Ra's al Ghul...to Batman's perfect reaction when he sees Wonder Woman's invisible jet ("He wants one." That is the exact right reaction.)...TRINITY lets every moment feel like the usually unattainable first time. Which is the entire point.

And as anyone who's read any of his other work knows, Wagner's specialty isn't just the small ideas—it's the big ones. The philosophical ones. The ones most writers of DC's trinity would never approach—like the moment where the darkest knight is overcome by Paradise, in the form of this wonderful woman, and that even this slightest taste of Perfection both taints and inspires him. Forever. Or the moment where Bizarro is both overwhelmed and confused by the Truth Diana's lasso demands—and their reactions as Truth is undone. These are not small ideas.

Even the art adds to the magic trick, keeping us so preoccupied with a visual bamboozle, we almost don't notice what's right in front of us. Forget the more Fleischer/Shuster-like Superman...or the short-eared Batman...or the regal posture on Wonder Woman. Those are obvious. Instead, look at the shot of Clark and Bruce in the limousine on pages 26 and 27. The calm playboy vs. the interrogating reporter. They're exact opposites of their alter-egos, but in the same breath, perfectly in character. Most important, even without the costumes, we know exactly who they are. With a lesser artist, the moment is lost. With a lesser writer, it's never even there to begin with. In life, most people are lucky to be great at one thing. Astoundingly, and to our benefit, Wagner is great at two.

Clark, Bruce and Diana are not simple characters. They're tough and unstoppable and vulnerable and perfect and flawed and kind and ruthless and noble and selfish and pure. They're as familiar as your own thumbnail, yet you still don't know everything about them. They're Superman, Batman and Wonder Woman. They're Clark, Bruce and Diana. They're icons. And, lucky us, they're in Matt Wagner's hands.

Prepare yourself. Watch carefully. Like the best magician, he makes it look so easy.

Brad Meltzer
Hollywood, Florida
February 2004

Brad Meltzer is the author of the New York Times *bestsellers* The Inner Circle, The Book of Fate, The Tenth Justice, Dead Even, The First Counsel, The Millionaires *and* The Zero Game, *among others. His DC Comics work includes* GREEN ARROW: THE ARCHER'S QUEST, IDENTITY CRISIS *and* JUSTICE LEAGUE OF AMERICA, *for which he won an Eisner Award.*

METROPOLIS.

WHERE THE TRAINS ALWAYS RUN ON TIME.
PLANET! DAILY PLANET! SUPERMAN ON PAGE ONE! DAILY PLANET!
WAIT!
EXCUSE ME, I... EXCUSE ME, UM...
NEED TO CATCH--
EASY, PAL!
SORRY, I--
WAIT!
I TRY TO MISS ONE AT LEAST THREE TIMES A WEEK.

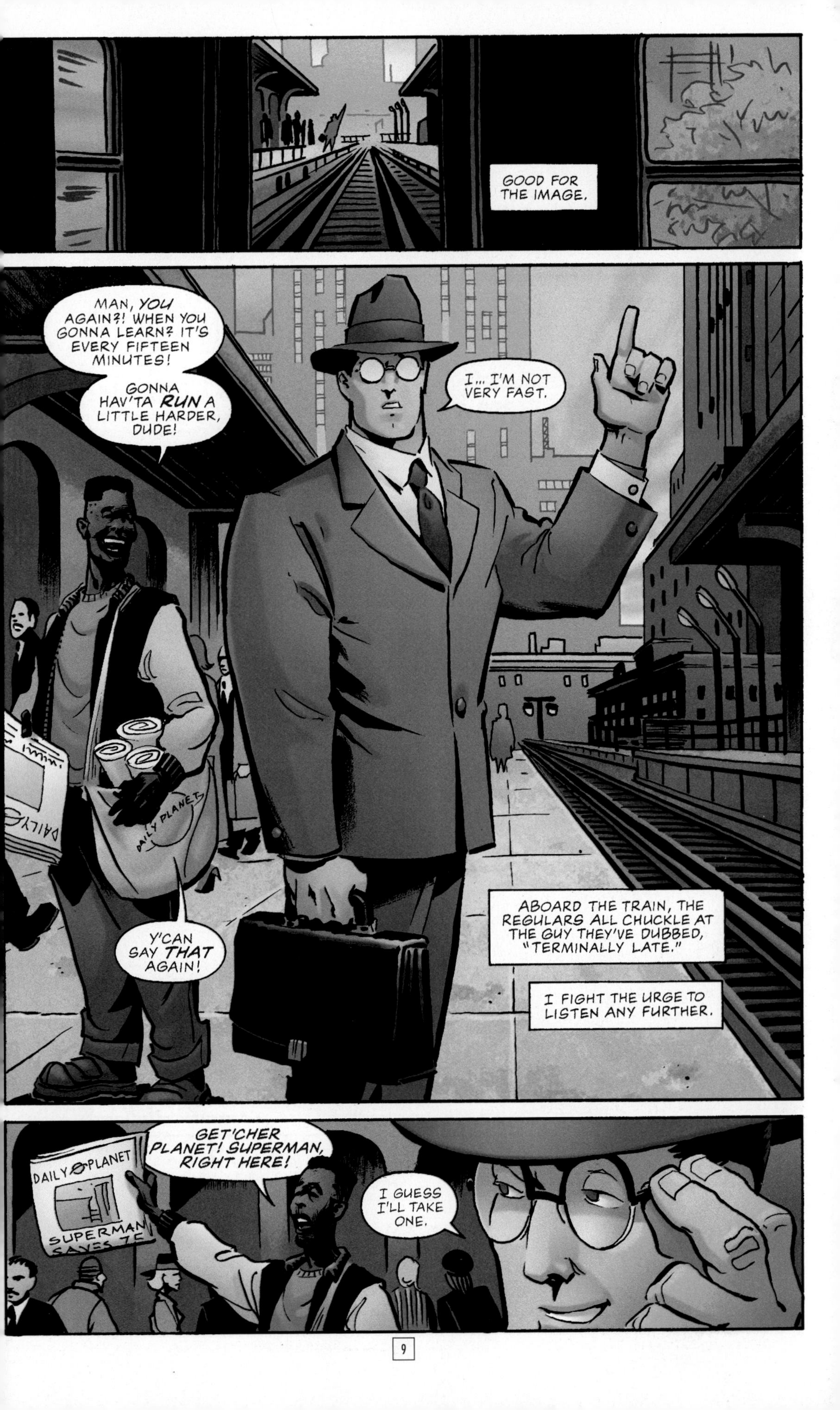
GOOD FOR THE IMAGE.
MAN, YOU AGAIN?! WHEN YOU GONNA LEARN? IT'S EVERY FIFTEEN MINUTES!
GONNA HAV'TA RUN A LITTLE HARDER, DUDE!
I... I'M NOT VERY FAST.
Y'CAN SAY THAT AGAIN!
ABOARD THE TRAIN, THE REGULARS ALL CHUCKLE AT THE GUY THEY'VE DUBBED, "TERMINALLY LATE."
I FIGHT THE URGE TO LISTEN ANY FURTHER.
DAILY PLANET
DAILY PLANET
SUPERMAN
GET'CHER PLANET! SUPERMAN, RIGHT HERE!
I GUESS I'LL TAKE ONE.

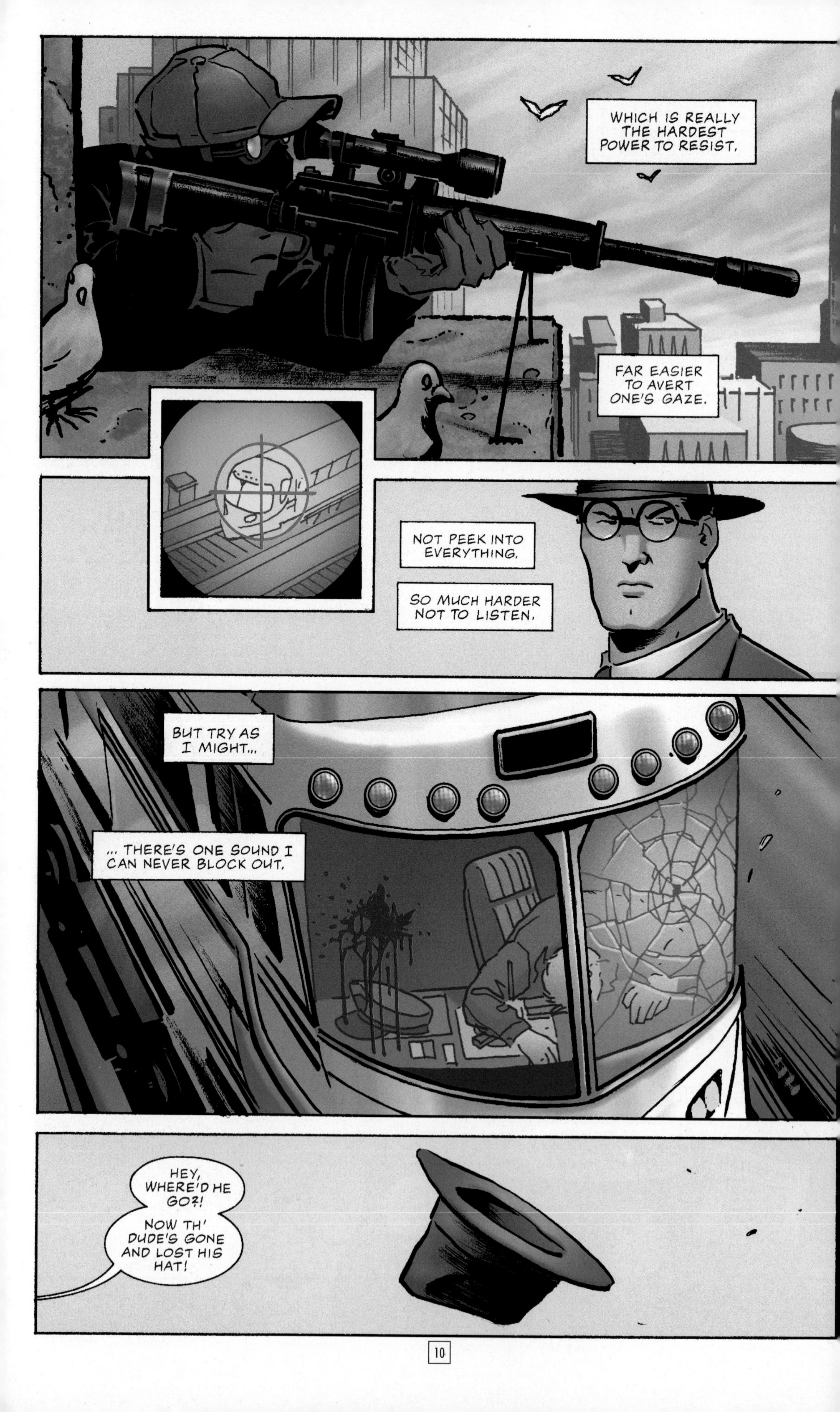
WHICH IS REALLY THE HARDEST POWER TO RESIST.
FAR EASIER TO AVERT ONE'S GAZE.
NOT PEEK INTO EVERYTHING.
SO MUCH HARDER NOT TO LISTEN.
BUT TRY AS I MIGHT...
... THERE'S ONE SOUND I CAN NEVER BLOCK OUT.
HEY, WHERE'D HE GO?!
NOW TH' DUDE'S GONE AND LOST HIS HAT!

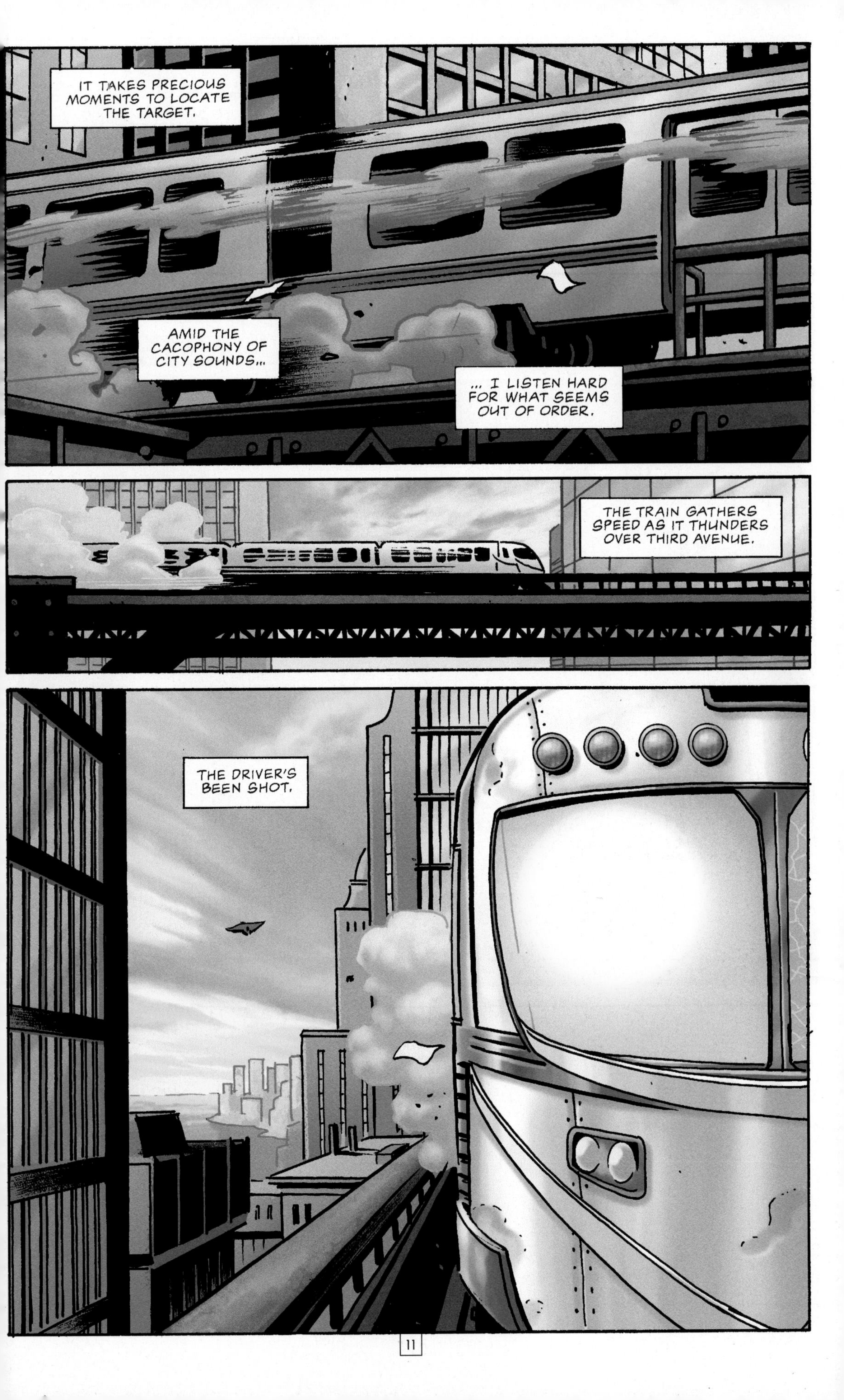
IT TAKES PRECIOUS MOMENTS TO LOCATE THE TARGET.
AMID THE CACOPHONY OF CITY SOUNDS...
... I LISTEN HARD FOR WHAT SEEMS OUT OF ORDER.
THE TRAIN GATHERS SPEED AS IT THUNDERS OVER THIRD AVENUE.
THE DRIVER'S BEEN SHOT.

AHEAD, A SHARP CURVE.
MUCH TOO FAST.
NEVER MAKE THE TURN.
NOW, OF COURSE, I HEAR...
... EVERY FRIGHTENED GASP...
... EVERY STUTTERING SCREAM.
THE TRAIN'S MOMENTUM IS ENORMOUS.
HOPE THIS WORKS...

THERE'S REALLY NO HANDBOOK FOR HOW TO DEAL WITH SUCH SITUATIONS.
TRY TO PULL ITS LURCHING MASS INTO THE CURVE.
DIDN'T WORK.
SHRIEKING METAL DROWNS OUT THE PASSENGERS.
MUST...
CATCH...
THAT...
TRAIN.

AS ALWAYS, ONE THOUGHT DRIVES ME ONWARD.
COMPELS BOTH MY CRUSADE AND MASQUERADE.

THE IDEA THAT DISASTER...
... CAN BE AVERTED.
HOLY COW, THIS IS HEAVY!

THE PASSENGERS ARE SHAKEN.
BUT ALIVE.
THE SHOT'S TRAJECTORY LEADS...

RESCUE TEAMS
CAN HANDLE IT NOW.

... HERE.
BUT THE
SNIPER'S
LONG GONE.
WITHOUT
A TRACE.

"FASTER THAN A
SPEEDING BULLET"?
NOT THIS TIME.

FIRST TIME.
THEY GOT LUCKY.
THE MAN OF STEEL, DRAWN OUT BY A SINGLE SHOT.
NO ROOM FOR FAILURE TONIGHT.
OR CAPTURE.
IF THEY MUST TERMINATE, A WARNING IS NEEDED.
ONLY ONE THING FLIES SO FAST AND SO LOW.
NOW THEY KNOW HIS FREQUENCY.
TIME TO GET TO WORK.

BUT, EXPECTING THE SUPERSONIC...
... THEY'RE UNPREPARED FOR SOMETHING SHADOWY.
AND SILENT.

"KMET NEWS-- LIVE AT THE SITE OF A FOILED BURGLARY ATTEMPT HERE AT S.T.A.R. LABS, WHERE AN ANONYMOUS PHONE TIP HAS LED AUTHORITIES TO DISCOVER A GROUP OF HIGH-TECH THIEVES THAT HAD, APPARENTLY, ALREADY BEEN SUBDUED.
"A POLICE SPOKESMAN ON THE SCENE HAD THIS TO SAY..."
"WELL, WE ASSUME WE HAVE SUPERMAN TO THANK FOR THIS BUST, ALTHOUGH HE DOESN'T USUALLY LEAVE THE PERPETRATORS SO, UM...
"... HOGTIED!"

PA ALWAYS SAYS, "TAKE SOME TIME FOR YOURSELF."

"YOU KNOW, CLARK, YOU CAN'T SOLVE ALL OF THE WORLD'S PROBLEMS ON YOUR OWN."
HERE, IN A SPECIAL PLACE ALL FOR MYSELF--
--I HONOR THE DATE I'VE CHOSEN AS MY CELESTIAL FATHER'S BIRTHDAY.
MY MOTHER'S FOLLOWS IN EXACTLY SIX MONTHS.
I KNOW MY PEOPLE WORE CLOAKS.
AMONG THE WRAPPINGS INSIDE MY LIFE-ROCKET WAS A CEREMONIAL ROBE. ADULT-SIZED.
I LIKE TO THINK THE WOMEN WORE THEM AS WELL.

WILL I EVER KNOW THEIR CHOICES FOR SENDING ME TO EARTH?
WILL I EVER KNOW THE REASONS FOR THEIR PLANET'S DEMISE?
I REALIZE I CAN'T SOLVE ALL THE WORLD'S PROBLEMS.
BUT THAT'LL NEVER STOP ME FROM TRYING.

ANTARCTICA.
THE OTHER SIDE OF THE PLANET.
WHEN THE WORLD'S MOST INFLUENTIAL MAN HAS SOMETHING HE WANTS TO HIDE.
HE HIDES IT WELL.
THE CREATURE'S MUTATED GENETICS ALLOW FOR MASSIVE LEVELS OF ENERGY ABSORPTION.

BUT AT A COST.
ITS CELLS' STRUCTURE BEGINS TO CALCIFY WITH THE RETENTION OF TOO MUCH SOLAR FORCE.
TO KEEP HIS CREATION IN CHECK, THE WORLD'S MOST INFLUENTIAL MAN NEEDED SOME PLACE COLD AND SECURE.

EXCELLENT!
GENTLEMEN, GO TO WORK.
SOME PLACE BEYOND THE REACH OF ANY RIVAL. BEYOND THE SUSPICIONS OF ANY FOE.

DAILY PLANET
BACK HOME, A GANG OF HIGH-TECH THIEVES ARE CAUGHT BY AN UNKNOWN HAND.
COULD METROPOLIS HAVE AN ALL-NEW GUARDIAN ON DUTY?
PLANET, KENT HERE.
I WAS IN TOWN LAST NIGHT. TRIED TO FIND YOU, BUT NO LUCK.
ALL THOSE FREQUENT FLYER MILES FINALLY ADD UP?
I SHOULD'VE GUESSED IT WAS YOU. WHAT, WITH THE "GIFT-WRAPPING" AND ALL...
I NEVER GUESS, KENT. DANGEROUS HABIT.
SERIOUSLY...
Y PLANET
"...WE NEED TO TALK."

"SO, WHAT BRINGS GOTHAM'S FAVORITE SON TO METROPOLIS?"
"ON THE TRAIL OF A CRIME, KENT. AS ALWAYS.
"THE LATEST LED ME TO A WELL-FUNDED AND EXCLUSIVE CARTEL THAT DEALS IN THE HIGH END OF HOMICIDAL MERCHANDISE.
"GUNS, PULSE WEAPONS, SOPHISTICATED EXPLOSIVES, TOXINS AND VIRAL SPORES, EVEN WEAPON-GRADE PLUTONIUM.
"YOU NAME IT, THEY CLAIM THEY CAN OBTAIN IT.
"THEY CALL THEMSELVES '*THE PURGE!*'
"SEVERAL DAYS AGO, I BUSTED ONE OF THEIR MAIN CELLS AND UNCOVERED THEIR SCHEME FOR BREAKING INTO S.T.A.R. LABS."
CLARK, THEY WERE AFTER THE KRYPTONITE.
I FOUND *THIS* ON ONE OF THEIR MEMBERS.
I DIDN'T HAVE TIME TO BREAK THE ENCRYPTION CODES, SO I THOUGHT I'D LEAVE IT ALL IN YOUR... SPEEDY HANDS.
IT HELPS IF YOU DON'T WEAR GLOVES.

SOMETHING TELLS ME IT'S STOLEN.
THIS IS A LEXCORP PROJECTS SECURITY DISC.
WHICH MEANS THEY'RE ALSO PLANNING TO STEAL SOMETHING FROM LUTHOR.
THAT COULD GET UGLY.
AT THE VERY LEAST.
AS I'M SURE YOU KNOW, LUTHOR'S GOT HIS HOOKS IN ALL MANNER OF ADVANCED MILITARY TECHNOLOGY.
IF THIS "PURGE" GETS ACCESS TO SOME OF THAT STUFF, IT COULD SPELL B-A-D N-E-W-S INDEED.

THANKS, BRUCE. I APPRECIATE ALL YOU'VE DONE. I'LL LET YOU KNOW WHATEVER I DISCOVER.
BUT I CAN TAKE CARE OF MYSELF, YOU KNOW. EVEN AGAINST KRYPTONITE.
ONLY MAKING SURE.
AND YOU WERE OUT OF TOWN, YES?
JUST A BIT OF A VACATION.
I KNOW WHAT HE'S THINKING.
"CRIME NEVER TAKES A VACATION."
BUT THERE'RE NO BEAUTIFUL SUNSETS WAY DOWN IN THAT CAVE, BRUCE.

CAN WE GET ON WITH THIS?
CERTAINLY, MY DEAR.
MY ASSOCIATES IN AMSTERDAM CLAIM THAT YOU ARE ONE OF THE MOST SKILLED WARRIORS THEY HAVE EVER SEEN.
QUITE A CLAIM FOR ONE SO YOUNG. I'M GUESSING SEVENT--
EIGHTEEN!
OF COURSE.
STILL, JUST A FLEDGLING, THOUGH.
LOOK, MYSTERY MAN, THIS CRAP IS GETTING BORING. YOU WANT A DEMO?
FINE.
BRING IT ON.
VERY WELL, LET IT BE SO.
NOW, THAT'S MORE LIKE IT!

SO...
...ENOUGH OF THIS AUDITIONING STUFF!
DO YOU HAVE WORK FOR ME OR DO I MOVE ON TO THE NEXT SECOND-RATE CAESAR WITH A BIG BANKROLL?
INDEED. I BELIEVE I CAN MAKE USE OF YOUR TALENTS, MY DEAR.
MY ORGANIZATION HAS RECENTLY SUFFERED AN UNWELCOME LOSS, AND YOUR ADDITION WILL SOOTHE THAT RIFT QUITE NICELY.
PEACHY.
SO, WELCOME TO THE PURGE, MISS...
...AH... WHAT WAS IT AGAIN?
A... D-- DIANA.
CALL ME DIANA.

WITHIN AN HOUR, I'VE CRACKED THE SECURITY CODES.
KNOCK, KNOCK! WHO'S THERE?
THE DISC CONCERNS A CERTAIN "PROJECT REPLICA."
AN EXPERIMENT THAT DIDN'T WORK OUT QUITE THE WAY LEX HAD PLANNED.
ONLY THE PLANET'S MOST TALENTED, DEDICATED, AND... LET'S JUST SAY IT...
... ALL AROUND HOTTEST REPORTER! WAIT'LL YOU HEAR THIS ONE...
A BRIEF FEELING OF SHAME WASHES OVER ME.
HEY, IS THAT--?
WHAT'S THE DEAL, SMALLVILLE?! YOU KNOW LEX IS MY BEAT! EVEN PERRY SAYS I GET FIRST DIBS ON--HEY!
SORRY, LOIS, IT ISN'T WHAT YOU THINK. JUST YESTERDAY'S NEWS.
CLAAARK! WHAT'RE YOU--
AND I SHUDDER TO THINK WHY ANYONE WOULD WANT TO STEAL... THAT!
I'LL... I'LL EXPLAIN LATER.

MUSCLES HARD AND STIFF.

THE AMBIENT LIGHT OF THE GLACIER HAD BARELY KEPT HIM HIM ALIVE.

IN SUCH A FEEBLE STASIS, HIS TROUBLED MIND REMAINED CALM.

SEDATE.

SINCE BEING RESCUED, THOUGH, HE HAS BEEN SLOWLY STRENGTHENED ON A STEADY DIET OF MOONLIGHT.

AND THE OCCASIONAL INFRARED BATH.

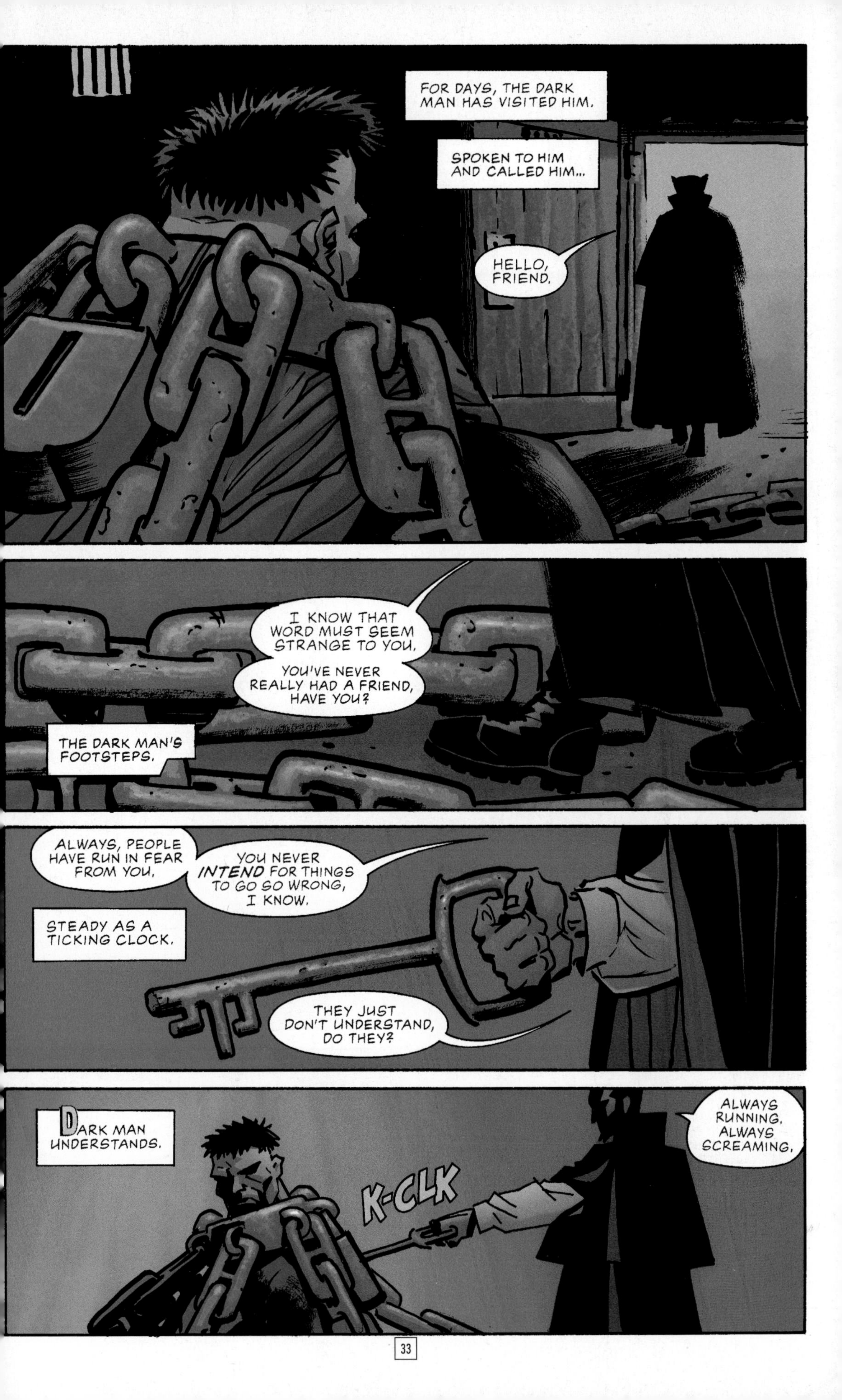
FOR DAYS, THE DARK MAN HAS VISITED HIM.
SPOKEN TO HIM AND CALLED HIM...
HELLO, FRIEND.
I KNOW THAT WORD MUST SEEM STRANGE TO YOU.
YOU'VE NEVER REALLY HAD A FRIEND, HAVE YOU?
THE DARK MAN'S FOOTSTEPS.
ALWAYS, PEOPLE HAVE RUN IN FEAR FROM YOU.
YOU NEVER INTEND FOR THINGS TO GO SO WRONG, I KNOW.
STEADY AS A TICKING CLOCK.
THEY JUST DON'T UNDERSTAND, DO THEY?
DARK MAN UNDERSTANDS.
ALWAYS RUNNING. ALWAYS SCREAMING.
K-CLK

CHANK
CHANK
CHANK
MY NAME IS RA'S AL GHUL AND I AM, INDEED, YOUR FRIEND.
IN FACT, YOUR EFFORTS, YOUR AID, YOUR SERVICE WILL BE INVALUABLE TO ME IN THE DAYS AHEAD.
I CANNOT THANK YOU ENOUGH.
I KNOW THAT, IN THE PAST, THINGS HAVE SEEMED... LESS THAN CLEAR TO YOU. RELAX, FRIEND, YOU'VE SUFFERED ENOUGH.
I'M HERE TO MAKE CERTAIN THAT NEVER HAPPENS AGAIN.
YOU ARE, IN FACT, MY MOST CHERISHED COMRADE.

THE SINGLE MOST IMPORTANT PART IN THE VAST SCOPE OF MY GLOBAL OPERATIONS.
YES, YOU, MY FRIEND...
... ARE MY NUMBER ONE!
DARK MAN AM BIZARRO'S FRIEND.
BIZARRO #1
NOW THEN... I HAVE A SMALL FAVOR OR TWO I'D LIKE TO ASK OF YOU.

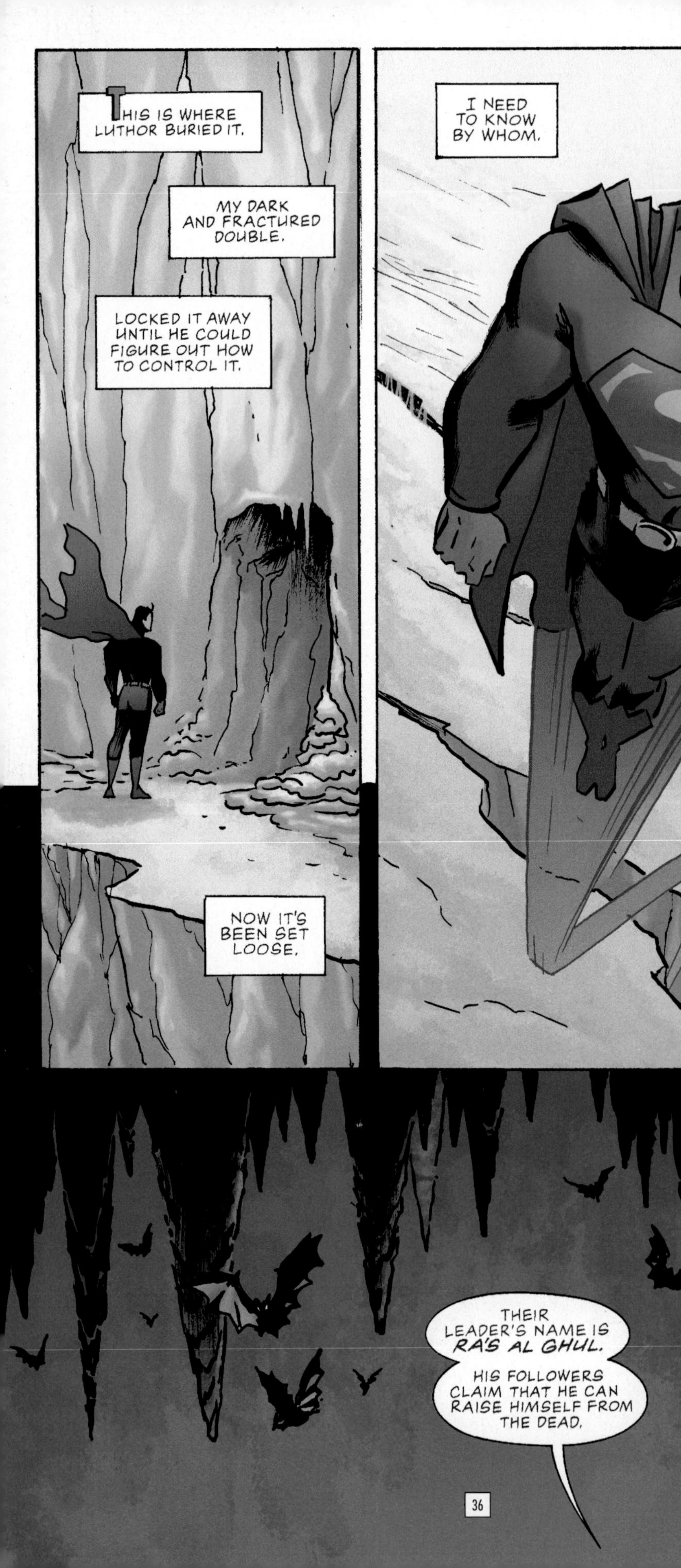
THIS IS WHERE LUTHOR BURIED IT.
MY DARK AND FRACTURED DOUBLE.
LOCKED IT AWAY UNTIL HE COULD FIGURE OUT HOW TO CONTROL IT.
NOW IT'S BEEN SET LOOSE.
I NEED TO KNOW BY WHOM.
THEIR LEADER'S NAME IS *RA'S AL GHUL.*
HIS FOLLOWERS CLAIM THAT HE CAN RAISE HIMSELF FROM THE DEAD.

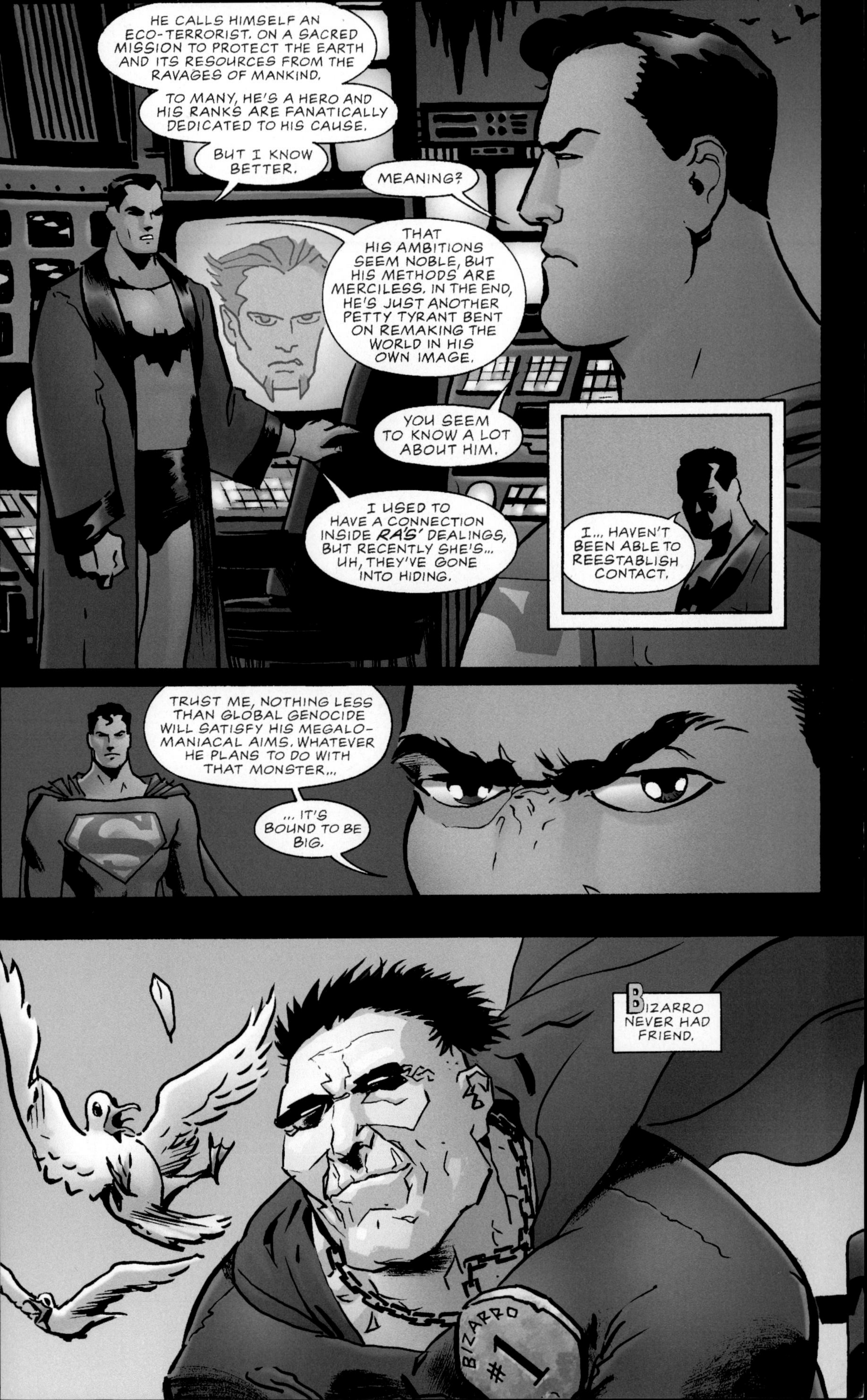
HE CALLS HIMSELF AN ECO-TERRORIST. ON A SACRED MISSION TO PROTECT THE EARTH AND ITS RESOURCES FROM THE RAVAGES OF MANKIND.
TO MANY, HE'S A HERO AND HIS RANKS ARE FANATICALLY DEDICATED TO HIS CAUSE.
BUT I KNOW BETTER.
MEANING?
THAT HIS AMBITIONS SEEM NOBLE, BUT HIS METHODS ARE MERCILESS. IN THE END, HE'S JUST ANOTHER PETTY TYRANT BENT ON REMAKING THE WORLD IN HIS OWN IMAGE.
YOU SEEM TO KNOW A LOT ABOUT HIM.
I USED TO HAVE A CONNECTION INSIDE RA'S' DEALINGS, BUT RECENTLY SHE'S... UH, THEY'VE GONE INTO HIDING.
I... HAVEN'T BEEN ABLE TO REESTABLISH CONTACT.
TRUST ME, NOTHING LESS THAN GLOBAL GENOCIDE WILL SATISFY HIS MEGALO-MANIACAL AIMS. WHATEVER HE PLANS TO DO WITH THAT MONSTER...
...IT'S BOUND TO BE BIG.
BIZARRO NEVER HAD FRIEND.
BIZARRO #1

BIZARRO'S NEW FRIEND AM COOL.

BIZARRO NEVER HAD COOL FRIEND.

"RACER COOL."
SUN AM BAD ON BIZARRO'S FACE.
BUT MAKE BIZARRO STRONG AGAIN.

TOO BAD HIM HELPERS BREAK SO EASY.
BIZARRO DIDN'T MEAN TO SHAKE ONE SO HARD.
THEN OTHER TWO TRIED TO GRAB BIZARRO.
BIZARRO DIDN'T MEAN TO SLAP OTHER TWO SO HARD.
RACER COOL SAY IT OKAY.
RACER COOL ASK FOR PAIR OF MISSILES.
BIZARRO BRING WHOLE THING.
RACER COOL SAY IT OKAY.

THE WIND IS FEROCIOUS.
BANG
INSIDE, HALF OF HIS CREW LIES DEAD OR INJURED.
PING
THE SUB HAD BEEN SHAKEN LIKE A BOX OF CANDY.
MEN SMASHED INTO STEEL, BROKEN LIKE DOLLS.
WHEN THEY HAD FIRST REALIZED THAT THEY WERE UNDER ATTACK...
... DEAR GOD...
... THEY'D ARMED AND LOADED A MISSILE.

SHELTERED FROM THE OUTSIDE WORLD, THE ISLAND LIES PEACEFUL INSIDE ITS MISTS.
THE SENTRIES CIRCLE ITS PEAKS.
READY TO SOUND THE ALARM IN CASE OF INTRUSION OR ATTACK.
READY TO CALL DOWN THE WRATH OF THE GODS.

"I AM NEITHER A ZEALOT NOR A MADMAN,"
"I AM A REALIST AT LEAST, AND A FUTURIST AT BEST."

SOME DO NOT AGREE.
THUS, WE MUST USE WHATEVER MEANS NECESSARY TO PRESERVE THAT WHICH THE REST OF MANKIND WOULD PILLAGE AND RAPE.
THE WORLD WILL THANK US SOMEDAY.
HERE, I THOUGHT YOU WANTED AN UPDATE ON TEAM-UNIT TRAINING.
IF YOU'RE NOT TOO BUSY "SAVING THE PLANET" THAT IS...
OF COURSE, MY DEAR.
YOUR REPORT, THEN...
HOW FARE MY FOLLOWERS?
WELL... THEY'RE ACTUALLY DOING QUITE WELL.
ENDURANCE TEST SCORES ARE UP, AND RESPONSE TIMINGS ARE MUCH IMPROVED. THEY'RE A TIGHT BUNCH.
THEY HAVE BELIEF IN THEIR VERY BONES.
DEVOTION DEEP IN THEIR FLESH.

I GOTTA ADMIT, YOU INSPIRE THEM. OR YOUR MESSAGE...
IT IS THE WORLD, ITSELF, THAT INSPIRES THEM.
EARTH IS A LONELY AND PRECIOUS THING. AND MANKIND HAS NEVER DONE ANYTHING BUT ABUSE IT.
MY FOLLOWERS UNDERSTAND THE DIRE NEED. IT'S TIME TO WIPE CLEAR THE GLOBAL PLATE OF CIVILIZATION AND ALL ITS TRAGEDIES.
TIME TO BEGIN THE WORLD ANEW WITH A FRESH PALETTE.
WHERE I COME FROM, THEY NEVER WORRY ABOUT THE REST OF THE WORLD AT ALL. ONLY THEIR OWN PROBLEMS...
AND WHERE MIGHT THAT BE, MY DEAR? I DON'T QUITE PLACE THE ACCENT...
A PLACE THE REST OF THE WORLD HAS ALL BUT FORGOTTEN...
...AND THEY LIKE IT THAT WAY.

WHEN I FIRST R-- LEFT HOME, I NEVER KNEW HOW COLD THE OUTSIDE WORLD COULD BE.
FOUND THE ONLY ASSETS I CARRIED WITH ME WERE THE CHANCE TO SELL MY BODY, AND THE ABILITY TO KICK WHO-EVER'S ASS MIGHT WANT TO TRY TO SELL IT FOR ME. ONE THING ABOUT WHERE I GREW UP...
BEATS NEVER KNOWING ANY DIFFERENT.
... A GIRL LEARNS TO TAKE CARE OF HERSELF.
AND SO NOW I'M A HIRED FIST.
YOU SELL YOURSELF SHORT, MY DEAR. IT TAKES TREMENDOUS COURAGE TO CONFRONT THE UNKNOWN.
ANY LESS VALOR AND SLAYER WOULD HAVE HAD YOUR HAND OFF BY NOW.
EFFENDI? A PROBLEM...
THE CREATURE HAS RETURNED.
SO... THIS IS YOUR FIRST TIME IN METROPOLIS?
Y'GOTTA MAKE SURE TO SEE ALL THE SIGHTS! NOW, I OFFER A COMPLETE CITY TOUR PACKAGE FOR ONLY--
THE SENTRIES' SCREAMS STILL ECHO ALONG THE CLIFFS.
HERE.
WHAT, THE PARK?
METRO CAB

YES, HERE WILL BE FINE. THANK YOU, DRIVER.
THEY REPORTED A FLYING MAN RESPONSIBLE FOR THE NEAR-CATASTROPHE.
STRONG ENOUGH TO CARRY A NUCLEAR SUB.
CLAD IN A RED CLOAK.
THE DESCRIPTION IS OBVIOUS.
I DO NOT RELISH THE CONFRONTATION THAT LIES AHEAD.
STILL, I HAVE LONG WISHED TO MEET THE MAN REPORTED TO BE STRONGER THAN HERCULES.
SWIFTER THAN HERMES.
BRAVER THAN ACHILLES.
BUT NOW...
...I NEED TO KNOW WHERE.

THE MONSTER'S HEARTBEAT SOUNDS LIKE BLUNTED THUNDER.
I CAN RECOGNIZE IT FROM MILES AND MILES AWAY.
STILL, MY EFFORTS TO "HEAR HIM OUT" HAVE SO FAR PROVEN FUTILE, EVEN AS FAST AS I DARE CRUISE WITHOUT FEAR OF MISSING IT...
THE TASK IS HARDER THAN SEARCHING FOR A NEEDLE IN A HAYSTACK. MUCH HARDER, ACTUALLY.
THAT, I CAN DO PRETTY QUICK.
SO FAR, I'M ONLY CERTAIN THAT IT ISN'T IN NORTH AMERICA.
TOMORROW, I'LL FINISH THE HEMISPHERE.
THEN, THE VASTNESS OF ASIA.

I WONDER HOW BRUCE ALWAYS MAKES IT LOOK SO EASY.
SUPERMAN...
I WILL ALWAYS REMEMBER MY FIRST SIGHT OF HER.
LOIS, YOU'RE THE MOST COMPELLING WOMAN I'VE EVER MET.

I GREET YOU IN PEACE.
MY NAME IS DIANA, EMISSARY AND AMBASSADOR FOR THE AMAZON PEOPLE.
I APOLOGIZE FOR THIS RATHER ABRUPT APPROACH, BUT... YOU'RE NOT EXACTLY AN EASY PERSON TO CONTACT.
AND... WE REALLY NEED TO TALK.
SMOOTH, DIANA.
HE'S LARGER THAN I IMAGINED.
BUT THIS... IS THE MOST MAGNIFICENT.

SHE'S... FLYING.
LIKE ME.
BEHIND HER... A PORTAL OF SOME SORT.
NOW I SEE, THE ENTRANCE TO SOME TYPE OF JET. STONE SILENT.
INVISIBLE TO NORMAL VISION.
JUST THIS MORNING, I KNOW YOU EXPERIENCED AN... ACCIDENT... WHILE ESCORTING A NUCLEAR SUBMARINE.
I'M NOT SUGGESTING THAT YOU DELIBERATELY CAUSED THE EXPLOSION. STILL, I'VE BEEN ASKED TO SPEAK WITH YOU ABOUT THE POSSIBLE REPERCUSSIONS OF SUCH CARELESSNESS.
I COME FROM AN ISLAND KNOWN AS THEMYSCIRA.
IT'S NOT ON ANY MAP, BUT I ASSURE YOU, IT LIES DANGEROUSLY NEAR TO WHERE THIS BLAST... OCCURRED.
I... I CAN EXPLAIN.

DAILY PLANET
... AND SO, I'VE BEEN TRYING TO LOCATE IT EVER SINCE.
I'M SO EMBARRASSED.
DON'T BE. IT'S AN HONEST MISTA--
YOU DON'T UNDERSTAND. TO MY PEOPLE, A FALSE ACCUSATION IS ALMOST AS BAD AS THE CRIME ITSELF.
RELIEF FLOODS THROUGH ME.
I SHOULD HAVE KNOWN.
AFTER ALL, HIS PASSION FOR JUSTICE SEEMS SO MUCH LIKE MY OWN.
NO HARM DONE. REALLY.
BUT I DON'T THINK THE ROOF-TOP OF A NATIONAL NEWS OUTLET IS THE BEST PLACE TO DISCUSS ALL THIS.
OH-- OF COURSE, YOU'RE RIGHT.
FOLLOW ME!
INSIDE THE JET.
HIDDEN FROM VIEW.
PLEASE, C'MON IN.

DON'T MIND THE MESS.
YOU SAY THIS... BIZARRE CREATURE IS IN THE THRALL OF A CULT LEADER OF SOME SORT. THEN HE MUST PLAN ON USING THE REMAINING ARMAMENT WITHIN THE SUB.
SUCH A MAN IS AN OBVIOUS MENACE TO ALL THE WORLD'S SECURITY.
I WILL JOIN YOU IN HIS PURSUIT.
THAT IS... I THINK I CAN HELP.
EASY DOES IT, PRINCESS...
THE JET'S SENSORS SHOULD BE ABLE TO TRACK THE SUB REACTOR'S RESIDUAL ION TRAIL.
DON'T KNOW WHY I DIDN'T THINK OF THAT BEFORE. I GUESS WE ALL JUST ASSUMED YOU HAD IT... WELL...
AGAIN, MY APOLOGIES.
AGAIN, FORGET IT. FIND ANY-THING?
YES, THE JET DETECTS AN UNUSUALLY STRONG ION STREAM, HEADING EASTWARD. CLOSE TO THE EQUATOR.
FOLLOW IT, THEN...

THIS TECHNOLOGY IS ALIEN. IS SHE AN ASTRAL IMMIGRANT AS WELL?
SHE IS A WARRIOR...
...AND A DIPLOMAT?
SURE, I'D APPRECIATE ANYTHING YOU CAN DO.
BUT, BEFORE WE GO, I HAVE A QUESTION...
HOW DID YOU KNOW WHERE TO LOCATE ME TONIGHT?
I JUST ASKED AROUND.
"HUMANS ARE EASY TO FOOL, AS YOU KNOW.
"BUT THE CITY BIRDS KNOW WHEN AND WHERE SOMETHING FLIES THROUGH THEIR AIRSPACE."

THE SAHARA DESERT.
THERE'S BEEN A RECENT EVACUATION HERE. THESE TENT POST HOLES AND TIRE TRACKS...
THE CREW'S BODIES ARE STILL INSIDE THE SUB. LONG DEAD, FROM THE LOOKS OF IT. AND YOU WERE RIGHT...
...ALL THE MISSILE RACKS ARE EMPTY.
AND THOSE ARE SAND SWIRLS FROM A HELICOPTER LANDING.
SEVERAL, ACTUALLY.
THIS CAMPSITE ISN'T LARGE ENOUGH TO HOUSE SUCH AN OPERATION.
BUT WHERE WERE THEY STATIONED?

TO GAZE INTO THE EARTH IS CONFUSING.
MURKY AND STUDDED WITH ELEMENTS THAT BLOCK MY SPECIAL SIGHT.
STILL, I SEARCH FOR EVIDENCE OF ORDER AND STRUCTURE.
THINGS MANMADE.

HE IS SO USED TO ACTING ALL ALONE.
WELL DONE. THIS WAS THEIR LAIR?
SEEMS SO. THE COMPLEX IS LARGE AND EXTENDS DEEP UNDERGROUND.
COULDN'T SEE MUCH ELSE. MOST OF THE DOORS AND WALLS CONTAIN A LEAD ALLOY.
I... HAVE TROUBLE SEEING THROUGH THAT.
HOW DO PEOPLE LIVE LIKE THIS? BURIED INSIDE THE EARTH?
I'VE NEVER ACTUALLY TOLD ANYONE THAT BEFORE.

DOWN THE TUNNEL, HE WALKS AHEAD OF ME. AS IF I NEED PROTECTION,
LOOKS LIKE THEY LEFT IN A HURRY, THERE'RE ENOUGH SUPPLIES HERE TO LAST FOR MONTHS.
UNLESS... THEY HAVEN'T ALL GONE.
I DON'T HEAR ANY BREATHING, BUT IF IT'S AN AMBUSH...
BUT--
SHHH... I'M CHECKING FOR HEARTBEATS.
DIANA! LOOK--
IN THE NAME OF THE DEMON!
BRADDA
BRAD BRADDA BRADDA BR

--OUT.
HE SEEKS TO WARN ME, BUT I RECOGNIZE THE TRAP.
SMELL THE OIL OF GUN BARRELS.
THE SWEATY STENCH OF FEAR.
SHE'S... FINE.
AND THEY'RE LUCKY.

SSSSSSSSS
UNIT A, FALL BACK!
UNIT B, ADVANCE!

THEY SWARM OVER US LIKE LOCUSTS.
WHAT IS THIS?
THE FRIENDLY DIVISION?
DIANA NOTICES FIRST.
SUPERMAN! THEY'RE SUICIDE BOMBERS!
COVERED IN GRENADES!
TOO MANY TO DISARM.
CHCK

...EVEN FOR A SPEEDING BULLET.
AGAIN, HE MOVES TO PROTECT ME.
SUCH A...MAN.
THESE SUPPORTS CAN'T TAKE MUCH MORE DAMAGE LIKE THAT.
FURTHER AHEAD... THERE'S ANOTHER LINE OF DEFENSE.
WHAT ARE THEY...?
SNIFF
WHAT MANNER OF DESPOT IS THIS? WHOSE DEVOTEES SO WILLINGLY EMBRACE THEIR OWN DEATHS...?

NERVE GAS!
THEN, OUT OF NOWHERE, LIKE ÆOLUS...
... HE SUMMONS A MIGHTY WIND.
MNPH--
sP-TOO!
UM... SORRY ABOUT THAT.
YOU SHOULD SEE MY SISTER...
IT'S TOO LATE FOR THESE SORRY SOULS.
AND THE TEAM LEADER'S LOCKED HIMSELF INSIDE THAT VAULT.
SHALL WE?

OH, MIGHTY DEMON...
... IT IS IN YOUR NAME THAT I NOW DO AS YOU BADE ME.
I PRAY MY ACT BRINGS HONOR TO BOTH THE HOUSE OF UBU AND OUR EXALTED MASTER.
WHAM!

HE WAS FALLING EVEN AS WE CRASHED THROUGH.
ONE MORE VICTIM OF THE PURGE.
BUT WE HAD BIGGER THINGS TO WORRY ABOUT.
IT'S BEEN ARMED.
QUICK, PULL THE WIRING!

TOO LATE. THE IGNITION SEQUENCE HAS BEGUN.
BUT... WHAT'LL WE...?
NO TIME TO FLY IT INTO SPACE! QUICKLY, GET AS FAR AWAY FROM THE ENTRANCE AS YOU CAN!
BUT...
NO! I CAN'T JUST LEAVE YOU HERE!
I WON'T!
NO TIME TO ARGUE-- GO!

AGAIN, HE MOVES TO PROTECT ME.
AS HE DOES EVERYONE.

AS I FLEE...
... AMONG THE DEBRIS...
... SOMETHING CAPTURES MY EYE.
PORT OF GOTHAM CITY
THIS BINDING...
PORT O
GOTHA
CITY
... IT'S AN AMAZON BRIDLE KNOT!
SURELY ONE OF US...
... CAN'T BE INVOLVED WITH ALL THIS MAD-NESS AND DEATH?

DEEP UNDER-GROUND, THE BLAST RUMBLES AND ROARS.
LIKE SOMETHING I HAVE HEARD FROM THE FAR SIDE OF TARTARUS.

SURELY NO ONE COULD SURVIVE SUCH A HOLOCAUST?

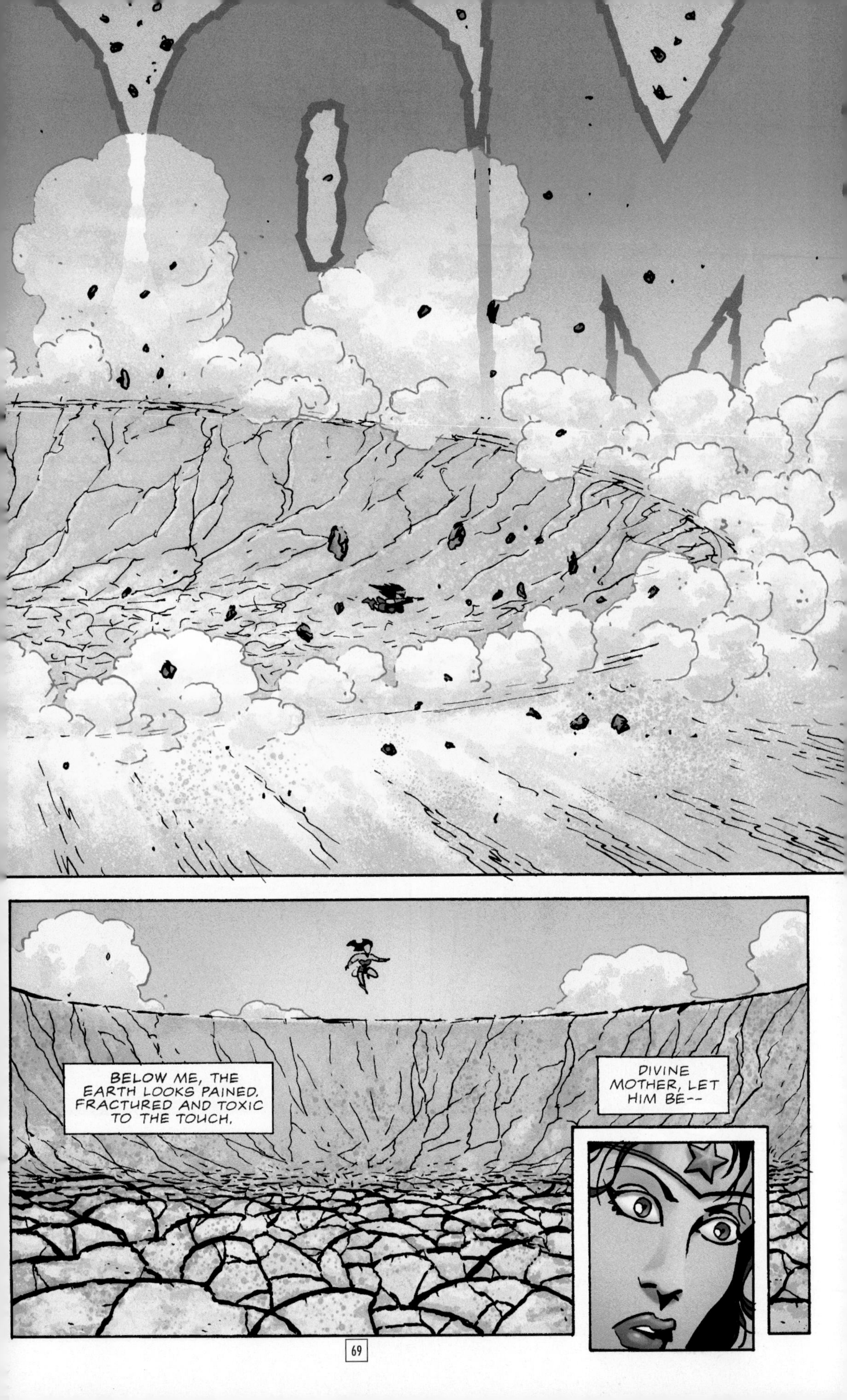
BELOW ME, THE EARTH LOOKS PAINED. FRACTURED AND TOXIC TO THE TOUCH.
DIVINE MOTHER, LET HIM BE--

THANK THE GODS! YOU'RE ALIVE! I FEARED...
WASN'T SO SURE MYSELF FOR A MOMENT THERE...
WHEW!
BUT WE'VE LOST ALL THE EVIDENCE. THEY'VE DESTROYED THE TRAIL.
ON THE WAY OUT, I SAW--
I... I SAW AN ABANDONED CRATE WITH A SHIPPING LABEL FOR THE PORT OF GOTHAM CITY.
NOT MUCH... BUT IT'S ALL WE'VE GOT. ALL RIGHT, THEN...
...ON TO GOTHAM.
I'VE GOT A FRIEND THERE WHO MIGHT BE ABLE TO HELP US.

GOTHAM.

WHERE CRIME NEVER SEEMS TO REST.
GOOD TO SEE YOUR ORGANIZATION IS ON TOP OF ITS GAME.
WE'VE BEEN TRYING TO SECURE SOME O'DIS TOP-SHELF FIREPOWER FOR MONTHS! YOU BIRDS IN D'PURGE MAKE IT ALL LOOK SO EASY.
HOPE YOU DON'T MIND IF WE...
...HEH--CHECK OUT THE MERCHANDISE?
SUIT YOURSELF, BUT DON'T GET ANY CRAZY IDEAS...
...OR YOU'LL LEAVE HERE WEARIN' THOSE BOXES, INSTEAD OF CARRYING THEM.
HE HAS SEEN FAR TOO MANY DIRTY DEALS LIKE THIS.

NICE.
OOH... I'M GETTIN' SWEATY ALL OVER!
PRIME STUFF, NO JOKE.
HEARD THE HORRIBLE CLATTER OF FAR TOO MANY BULLETS AND GUNS.
THUD! KRAK! WUMPH! THWAK!
TH' HELL--?!
AND SO, HE FIGHTS.
FOR JUSTICE.
SO THAT NO OTHER NEED HEAR THE ECHOES THAT HAUNT HIS DREAMS.
HE ACTUALLY ENJOYS THE PAINFUL SILENCE THAT WILL FOLLOW.
HE DOESN'T ASK FOR THEIR SURRENDER.
ITZAT-- BATFREAK!
OH, YEAH?!
HOW--?

WELL, ICE HIS FREAKY ASS!
THEY NEVER DO, ANYWAY.
THE CRAVEN.
AND THE FOOLISH.
ALL FIND UNDAUNTED COURAGE WITH A GUN IN THEIR HANDS.
HE HAS TRAINED A LIFETIME TO PROVE THEM WRONG.

PANG!

THIRTY-TWO SECONDS.
BUT, YOU WANNA RUMBLE...
ALL RIGHT, SPOOKY-PANTS,
DON'T KNOW HOW YOU TOOK OUT MY CREW LIKE THAT.
TO DISPATCH A ROOMFUL OF ARMED AND DANGEROUS MEN.

...YOU GOT IT!

NOW, ONLY A SLENDER YOUNG GIRL OPPOSES HIM.

KRAK!
STRANGE, SHE USES NO GU--

A LUCKY SHOT.
YOU WON'T GET ANOTHER.
THIS IS YOUR ONLY WARNING... DROP THE BATON AND YIELD.
YOU HEARD ME... THINK YOU'RE SO FREAKIN' TOUGH?
FORGET IT, CREEP!
WELL, BRING IT ON!
UNGH!
CHOK!

HER REFLEXES ARE SWIFT AND SEVERE.
HER TRAINING, ACUTE.
OOF!
WOK
UNGH!
BEFORE THE SLUDGY DARKNESS CLEARS FROM HIS HEAD, SHE'S GONE.
LEAVING BEHIND THE GUNS, AND THE LOOT.
AND HER CREW.

UNGHH... WH-WHERE...?
AH! AH! AGHHHH!
THE YOUNG VIXEN PLACES TOO MUCH FAITH IN HER TROOPS' ABILITY TO SELF-TERMINATE.
TOO LITTLE IN HIS GRITTY RESOLVE TO GET THE INFORMATION HE WANTS.
DON'T BOTHER GRINDING.
YOU'RE ON A NEW DENTAL PLAN. I'M AFRAID I HAD TO REMOVE THAT CYANIDE MOLAR.
THERE IS N-NO PATH BUT THE DEMON'S PATH! TH-THERE IS NO FEAR SAVE FOR HIS MIGHTY WRATH!
YOU DON'T SAY.
WHERE IS RA'S AL GHUL?
WHAT DO YOU KNOW OF PROJECT NOVA?
I WILL NEVER BETRAY THE ALMIGHTY DEMON!
I FEAR NO RETRIBUTION NOR DEATH.

YOU DON'T KNOW THE MEANING OF FEAR. BUT I'M HERE TO TEACH YOU.
EVER SEE A BODY DROPPED FROM THIRTY STORIES? YOU'LL MAKE A GREASY STAIN EVEN YOUR MOTHER WOULDN'T RECOGNIZE.
LAST CHANCE, MONKEY BOY! WHAT IS THE DEMON'S GOAL?!
I WILL NOT-- W... W...
TH-THE DEMON BRINGS DESTRUCTION IN HIS WAKE...
TH-TH-THIS CITY IS THE HOME OF HIS GREATEST FOE.
H-HE ALWAYS BRINGS DEATH TO THOSE--
THE TRUTH.
--THOSE WHO OPPOSE HIMMM...
TOO SIMPLE.
LIKE SOME MAGIC TRICK...

BRUCE ALWAYS SEEMS SURPRISED THAT I'M ABLE TO LOCATE HIM SO EASILY.
THERE ARE OTHER-- MORE MERCIFUL--WAYS TO GO ABOUT THAT!
I DON'T HAVE TIME FOR MERCY.
AND I DON'T ASK FOR APPROVAL.

WE'RE NOT HERE TO INTERFERE WITH YOUR METHODS.
WE'VE COME TO ASK FOR YOUR HELP. BATMAN, I'D LIKE TO INTRODUCE--
LIKE I CAN'T HEAR THAT BELTFUL OF TRACKING DEVICES.
THE SO-CALLED "WONDER WOMAN."
I'VE HEARD REPORTS OF YOUR RECENT APPEARANCE AND ACTIVITIES.
I ASSUMED SHE WAS RELATED TO YOU. MAYBE A DISTANT COUSIN.
AREN'T YOU A BIT UNDERDRESSED FOR ALL THIS?
AND WHY ARE YOU WEARING A MASK WHILE YOU TERRORIZE THIS MAN? ASHAMED TO SHOW YOUR FACE?!
WHOA! WHOA! TAKE IT EASY!
THIS COULD CERTAINLY GO BETTER.
BATMAN, WE'VE COME BECAUSE OF THE PURGE.

HE LISTENS WITH A PREDATOR'S EAR, ABSORBING EVERY FACT, PROCESSING IT FOR THE HUNT.
WHY HASN'T THIS THEFT BEEN DISCOVERED? WHY WASN'T THE EXPLOSION DETECTED?
IT WAS A SOVIET SUB. THEY'RE NOTORIOUSLY SLOW TO ADMIT ANY DEFEAT, AND THE BLAST TOOK PLACE IN THE BERMUDA TRIANGLE.
AS YOU KNOW, THERE'S OFTEN RADIO INTERFERENCE IN THAT AREA.
THE QUESTION IS, WHAT DO WE DO ABOUT IT? HOW DO WE FIND THE REMAINING MISSILES?
RA'S IS A MADMAN, BUT HE'S NO FOOL. HE'LL MAKE FULL USE OF THE POWER NOW IN HIS HANDS.
HE'S ALWAYS HELD A SPECIAL... REGARD FOR MY ENMITY. IN A SENSE, NO ONE KNOWS HIM BETTER THAN I DO.
WE STILL HAVE A PRISONER. I SAY LET'S QUESTION HIM TO THE FULLEST.
BUT, I GET TO ASK THE QUESTIONS.
WELL... SO LONG AS YOU AGREE NOT TO MISTREAT HIM.
ALL RIGHT.
HOW'S IT WORK?
JUST GRIP THE LINE AND ASK. IT'S IMPOSSIBLE FOR HIM TO LIE.
LIKE SOME MAGIC TRICK.

WHAT IS YOUR RANK IN THE PURGE?
I-INFANTRY. GROUND EXCURSIONS AND LOCAL SECURITY.
SO, YOU KNOW WHERE RA'S' HEAD-QUARTERS ARE?
O-ONLY THE BARRACKS. H-HIS REAL ENCLAVE IS H-HIDDEN UNDER-GROUND.
D-D-DEEP BENEATH THE CITY.
WHAT IS HIS PLAN?
I D-DON'T KNOW...
WHAT ABOUT THE STOLEN MISSILES? WHERE HAS HE TAKEN THEM?
ONE... ONE OF THEM HAS BEEN BROUGHT HERE ...TO GOTHAM.
WHERE?
D-DON'T KNOW...
AND THE OTHERS?
S-SENT AWAY. N-NOT HERE...
DON'T KNOW WHERE THE OTHERS... ARE...
PL-PLEASE... MY STOMACH HURTS...
ALL DONE, THEN?
Y-YES...
YOU SURE?
Y-YES...
GOOD BOY!
KRAK!
SOMEWHERE BELOW...

GREETINGS, ANCIENT SYBIL.
HOW FARE THE MISTS OF KNOWLEDGE?
THIS PIT IS FULL AND RIPE, O DEMON.
... HIS ENEMY AWAITS.
ITS VAPORS RACE THROUGH MY MIND.
STILL, HER BODY SPASMS AS SHE DEEPLY INHALES...
... THE FUMES OF A LAZARUS PIT.
THE SEER'S BONES ARE STIFF WITH AGE.
THIS...
THIIIS PIT IS AN ENCHANTED CANKER WHERE THE LEY LINES CONVERGE! ITS VIGOR IS ASTOUNDING!
SO, THE CONVERGENCE IS STILL ON DUE COURSE?
THE STRESS OF ITS ROILING POWER HAS CAUSED A RIFT, HERE IN THE SUURROUNDINNG EARTH!
AND AS BELOW, SO BE IT ABOVE.
AS BELOW, SO BE IT ABOVE!

BUT, BEWARE, O DEMON!
THREE, YOU SAY?
PERHAPS THE DETECTIVE HAS TAKEN ON A PARTNER.
YOU ARE PURSUED BY A TRIAD OF FORMIDABLE FORCE!
STRENGTH, STEALTH AND SKILL THEY WIELD SUCH AS THE WORLD HAS NEVER SEEN!
THE OTHER, I EXPECTED, SOONER OR LATER.
DARLING, SYBIL, MY THANKS.
...MY SOUL FOR YOU, O DEMON.
MY LIFE...
AS IT HAS ALWAYS BEEN...
<GOOD BYE, OLD MOTHER. THE PEACE OF THE GODS BE WITH YOU.>
<BLESS YOU, CHILD. AND FARE YOU WELL.>
AGAIN, YOU SURPRISE ME... ONE SO YOUNG, WHO SPEAKS THE ANCIENT TONGUE...?
ONLY A BIT. WHERE'D YOU PICK HER UP?
JALEEL HAS BEEN WITH ME SINCE THE AGE OF NINE. HER WISE VISIONS HAVE OFTEN AIDED MY PURPOSES.
NINE?! BUT THAT'D MAKE YOU--?
YES.
OLDER THAN I APPEAR. AND THEN SOME.
THE DEMON'S LAUGHTER ECHOES OFF THE STONE AND STEEL.
THE PIT GURGLES IN REPLY.

YOU--YOU BRUTE!
YOU BROKE THE JAW OF A HELPLESS CAPTIVE!
NOW--
WAIT--
HOW DARE YOU USE AN INSTRUMENT OF TRUTH FOR SUCH MALICIOUS ENDS.
SO HELP ME...
ENOUGH!
HOW DO WE EVEN KNOW YOUR LITTLE ROPE TRICK REALLY WORKS?
SEEMS TO ME THE LEADER OF THIS CREW BORE A STRIKING RESEMBLANCE TO YOUR WHOLE SCENE.
EVEN WORE AN EAGLE CREST AND STARS.
WHA--?
I-I DON'T KNOW WHAT YOU MEAN.
NO AMAZON WOULD EVER BE PART OF SUCH A CULT.
REALLY.
SMOOTH, PRINCESS.

LISTEN, LADY!
DON'T LIKE IT? WELL, TOUGH!
JUST--
DON'T COME INTO MY TOWN AND START TELLING ME HOW IT'S DONE!
HOLD ON--
I OUGHTTA...
RIGHT.
LOOK, GOTHAM IS MY TURF!
IF THERE'S A MISSILE HERE, I'LL FIND IT AND DISARM IT! AND DEAL WITH RA'S AL GHUL!
WHY DON'T YOU TWO GET BUSY ON LOCATING THE OTHER ONES, YES?

BRUCE, WHY DOES IT ALWAYS HAVE TO BE SO DIFFICULT?
THIS IS YOUR FRIEND?
YEEEAH-- SORRY ABOUT THAT.
HE'S JUST NEVER BEEN MUCH OF A TEAM PLAYER.
LOOK, LET ME GO TALK TO HIM ALONE. I'M CERTAIN HE CAN...
I'M CERTAIN THAT WE CAN LOCATE THIS VILLAIN ON OUR OWN.
BUT NOWHERE NEARLY AS FAST. YOU DON'T UNDERSTAND. THIS GUY CAN FIND ANYTHING.
WAIT FOR ME. I KNOW WHERE HE'S PROBABLY HEADED. I'LL BE BACK SOON.
OOOOH, VERY WELL. HERE...
...IT'S A TRANSMITTER. I'LL BE IN THE JET.
THANKS.

UM, RA'S...?
I'VE BEEN MEANING TO ASK YOU... YOUR GUY THERE, UBU...?
DIDN'T WE LEAVE HIM AND A STRIKE TEAM BURIED ALIVE OUT IN THE DESERT?
THAT WAS HIS COUSIN. ALSO AN UBU.
UBU AND HIS CLAN HAVE SERVED MY CAUSE FOR GENERATIONS.
EACH MALE CHILD IS TRAINED TO SOMEDAY TAKE HIS PLACE AT MY SIDE. TO GIVE HIS LIFE, IF NECESSARY, IN SACRIFICE FOR MY OWN.
WHAT ABOUT THE WOMEN?
THE WOMEN ARE NEEDED TO NURTURE THE WARRIORS.
THEY ARE A PROUD AND PIOUS FAMILY. ONLY THE DESERT BREEDS SUCH EXCELLENCE.
THESE WESTERN CITIES, THEY CONSTRAIN MY DESIRES AND DAMPEN MY MIND.
I LONG FOR THE PURITY OF THE DESERT'S FLOWING DUNES.
THE TUNDRA'S GLACIAL PLAINS, THE WINDSWEPT VISTA OF THE STEPPES...

Y-YOU'RE SO RIGHT. MAKES ME... HMM...
NEVER THOUGHT I'D ACTUALLY FEEL... HOME-SICK.
AND WHERE, EXACTLY, IS HOME, DEAR? SOME PLACE SPARE AND SEVERE?
ACTUALLY, UM... NO. I--I COME FROM A TROPICAL ISLAND KNOWN AS THEMYSCIRA. I KNOW, WHY WOULD I LEAVE, HUH?
IT'S PRACTICALLY A PARADISE!
EVERYONE SAYS SO.
RELAX, MY DEAR, YOUR REASONS ARE YOUR OWN.
AND SOON, THIS URBAN BLIGHT WILL BE TOPPLED AND ALL THE WORLD WILL BECOME A PARADISE.
WITHOUT THE WEIGHTY ISSUES OF OBLIGATION AND HOME.
IT'S JUST... WHERE I COME FROM, YOU'RE SUPPOSED TO BE A CERTAIN WAY. GRACIOUS AND FORGIVING.
I'VE NEVER BEEN VERY GOOD AT EITHER.
I UNDERSTAND, DEAR.
YOU SOUND JUST LIKE MY DAUGHTER.
D-DAUGHTER?!

HER NAME IS TALIA.
AND SHE, TOO, ISN'T VERY FORGIVING.
BUT NOW, TO THE TASK! THE HOUR APPROACHES AND WE MUST ALL BE PREPARED. SEE THAT THE SQUAD LEADERS STAND READY.
THE VESSEL'S FULL CAPACITY WAS HALF A DOZEN LONG-RANGE MISSILES. THAT MEANS HE'S GOT FOUR LEFT.
FAR BELOW THE STATELY MANOR HOUSE IS WHERE BRUCE WAGES HIS WAR UPON CRIME.
HE ALWAYS SEEMS TENSE WHENEVER I'M HERE.
IT'S HIS PRIVATE PLACE.
TWO DAYS AGO, I BUSTED A PURGE COMMUNICATIONS CELL AND ACCESSED THEIR COMPUTER FILES, WHEREIN I DISCOVERED SOMETHING CALLED "PROJECT NOVA."
SOMETIME WITHIN THE NEXT TWENTY-FOUR HOURS, NINETY-FIVE PERCENT OF THE WORLD'S COMMUNICATIONS SATELLITES WILL PASS WITHIN FIVE CUBIC MILES OF EACH OTHER IN SPACE.

IT'S A FREAK CONVERGENCE OF THEIR ORBITAL TRAJECTORIES THAT WON'T HAPPEN AGAIN FOR THOUSANDS OF YEARS. I'M NOT EVEN SURE MANY WORLD LEADERS ARE AWARE OF IT.
YET SOMEHOW, RA'S NOT ONLY KNEW, BUT WAS PLANNING AN ATTACK.
IF HE DETONATES A WARHEAD IN THE CENTER OF THIS BUNCHING, IT'LL DISRUPT ALL GLOBAL COMMUNICATIONS, EFFECTIVELY THROWING THE WORLD INTO A TOTAL INFORMATION BLACKOUT.
TO LAUNCH A MISSILE THAT FAR INTO THE STRATOSPHERE, HE'D NEED A FULL SILO FACILITY.
OR BIZARRO.
I DOUBT IT. ONLY AN HOUR AGO, RADIO FREE EUROPE REPORTED AN ARMED ATTACK ON A SILO IN EASTERN BULGARIA.
OBVIOUSLY, THIS IS SOMETHING THAT I CAN'T HANDLE ALONE.
BRUCE, THAT'S BRILLIANT. BUT WHY DIDN'T YOU MENTION ALL THIS EARLIER?
I MEAN-- I KNOW YOU'VE HAD SOME TROUBLE WITH WOMEN IN THE PAST--
YOU KNOW NEXT TO NOTHING ABOUT ME, KENT.
I WASN'T SURE HOW HE'D PLANNED TO STRIKE UNTIL I HEARD ABOUT THE MISSILES.
AND I... JUST PREFER TO WORK ALONE, THAT'S ALL.

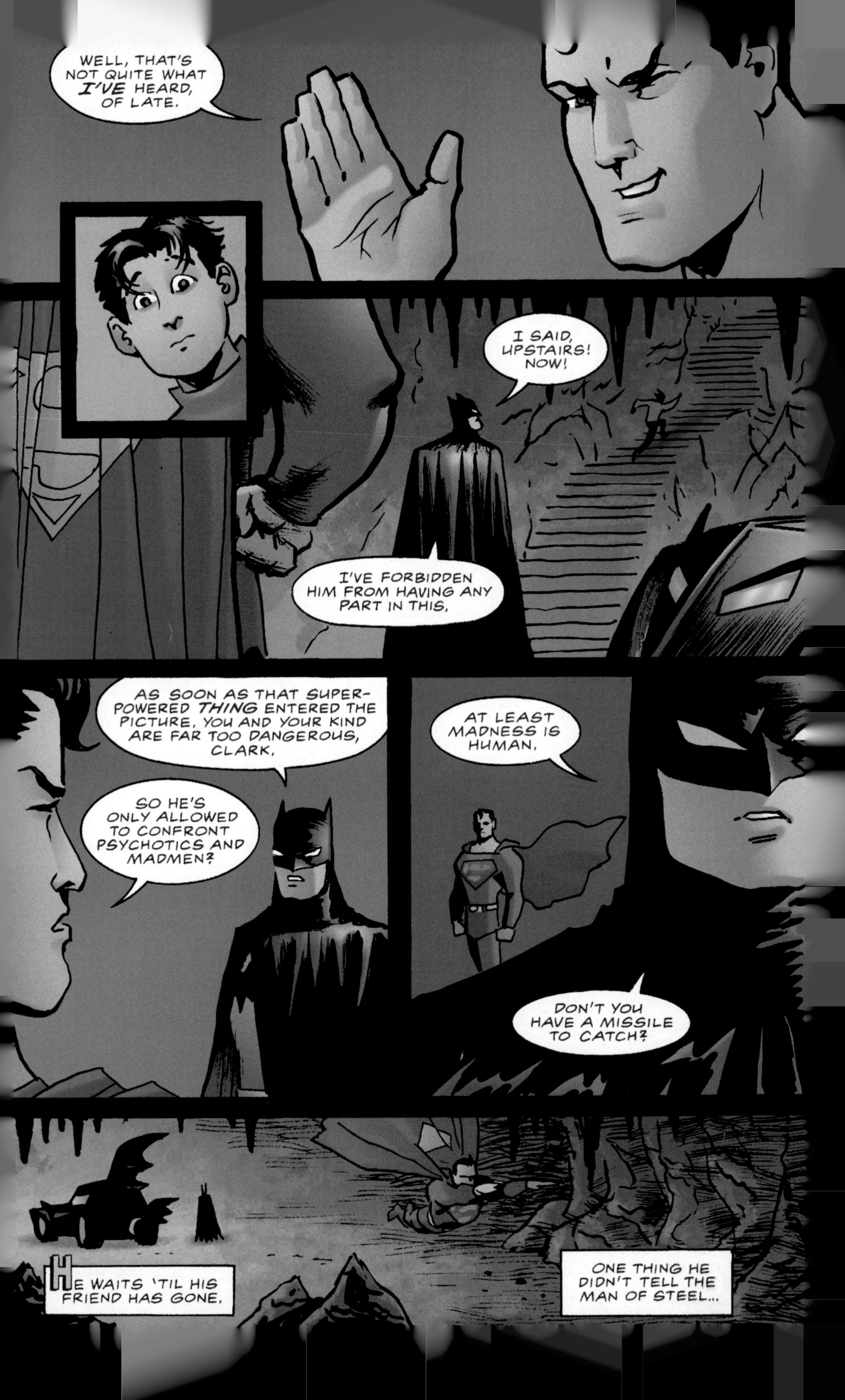
WELL, THAT'S NOT QUITE WHAT *I'VE* HEARD, OF LATE.
I SAID, UPSTAIRS! NOW!
I'VE FORBIDDEN HIM FROM HAVING ANY PART IN THIS.
AS SOON AS THAT SUPER-POWERED *THING* ENTERED THE PICTURE, YOU AND YOUR KIND ARE FAR TOO DANGEROUS, CLARK.
SO HE'S ONLY ALLOWED TO CONFRONT PSYCHOTICS AND MADMEN?
AT LEAST MADNESS IS HUMAN.
DON'T YOU HAVE A MISSILE TO CATCH?
HE WAITS 'TIL HIS FRIEND HAS GONE.
ONE THING HE DIDN'T TELL THE MAN OF STEEL...

...HE ALREADY KNOWS WHERE TO FIND RA'S AL GHUL.
MEN LOVE THEIR LITTLE SECRETS.
THEIR PRIVATE DENS, HIDDEN ENTRANCES, AND COVERT OPERATIONS.
STILL, IF I HADN'T BEEN LEFT BEHIND...
... I WOULDN'T BE PERFECTLY POSITIONED FOR THE JET'S RADAR TO PICK UP AN *UNUSUAL* FLYING OBJECT.
ONLY ONE THING TRAVELS SO SWIFT AND SO...
... CROOKED?

THE CREATURE'S PATH LEADS TOWARDS THE EASTERN, INDUSTRIAL PART OF THE CITY.
IN THE BLINK OF AN EYE, HE IS GONE.
I SHOULD WAIT FOR SUPERMAN, BUT THERE'S NO TELLING WHERE THE CREATURE HAS GONE.
ALONE, I DESCEND INTO THIS DEN OF MURDERERS AND THIEVES.

THE CREATURE IS GONE, BUT ITS LINGERING ODOR REMAINS.
LIKE SINGED OXYGEN AND MINERAL SALTS.
SOON ENOUGH, I CONFRONT A FAMILIAR SIGHT.
DON'T WANT THE WHOLE PLACE UP IN ARMS, JUST YET.
LIKE ODYSSEUS, I STEAL SILENTLY THROUGH THE OGRE'S CAVE...

THERE ARE OTHERS.
AND STILL MORE.
WHEN THE GUARD GROWS HEAVIEST, I CAN TELL I NEAR MY GOAL.
A REPORT, OH, DEMON, FROM OUR BROTHERS IN THE EAST.
THE SOVIET TROOPS HAVE BREACHED THE OUTER DEFENSES, BUT THE MISSILE IS PREPPED AND READY.
THEN LET THEM LAUNCH! AND REJOICE!
TELL THE TEAM TO TERMINATE ONLY AFTER THEY SEE IT FLY.
THEIR SOULS WILL FOLLOW IT INTO HEAVEN!
THIS IS A SACRED DAY, UBU...
PRAISE BE, THE RA'S AL GHUL. HIS WILL BE DONE!
IT IS HE.

IT WILL BE REMEMBERED WITH THE DAWNING OF A NEW WORLD.
EH...?
SELF-SANCTITY HAS ALWAYS BEEN THE CLAIM OF HISTORY'S MADMEN AND FOOLS!
YOU STRIKE ME AS A PRIME EXAMPLE OF BOTH, GHUL.
HA! YOU DON'T SAY?
UBU, INCAPACITATE THIS... COLORFUL YOUNG WOMAN. HAVE HER BOUND AND BROUGHT TO MY CHAMBERS.
SHE SHOULD PROVIDE SEVERAL HOURS OF AMUSEMENT BEFORE WE MUST FLY.

UNGH!
KRAK!
I FEEL HIS JAWBONE SHATTER ON THE END OF MY FIST.
IN ANGER, I STRIKE FAR HARDER THAN INTENDED.
AGGH!
ENOUGH OF THIS MADNESS!
YOUR LITANY OF TERROR IS OVER!
H-HELP ME, FRIEND...

THE COLLISION IS SO SUDDEN.
NO TIME TO REACT.
I HAVE NEVER FELT SUCH A BLOW.
TH-THANK YOU, AS ALWAYS, MY FRIEND.
NOW... CAN YOU BRING ME HER DEAD BODY? PLEASE?
MY HEAD THROBS LIKE THUNDER.
I SHRUG IT OFF.

MUST PRESS THE ATTACK.
KEEP HIM OFF BALANCE.
EVEN SO...
UNGH!
...IT'S LIKE PUNCHING THE AEGIS, ITSELF.
AND SO FAST.
I, WHO CAN DODGE BULLETS...
...BARELY SAW THE WHITE FLASH OF HIS FIST.

THE CREATURE GRUNTS AS THE LASSO HOLDS FAST.
TIGHTER. STRONGER EVEN THAN THE ICY TONS OF HIS GLACIAL TOMB.
CONFUSED.
ITS FRACTURED BRAIN IS BOMBARDED BY AN OVERWHELMING URGE...
... SOMETHING OF WHICH IT CAN MAKE NO SENSE.
THE AWFUL, UNTHINKABLE CONCEPT OF...
... TRUTH!

DIVINE MOTHER, I WITNESS CHAOS UNBOUND!
AS, WITH A TITAN'S ROAR...
...THE MONSTER BREAKS THE UNBREAKABLE!
HIS FURY IS EARTH-SHAKING.
SO FAST...
...I DIDN'T...
...COULDN'T...

BIZARRO NO LIKE GOLDEN BUGS IN HEAD.
NO LIKE LADY WITH ROPE.
LADY WITH ROPE BROKE BIZARRO'S BADGE!
BIZARRO AM RACER COOL'S NUMBER ONE FRIEND!
BIZARRO AM NUMBER ONE!

I HOPE DIANA'S ALL RIGHT.
TRIED TO CONTACT HER, BUT HAVE RECEIVED NO REPLY.
I ARRIVE JUST IN TIME AS THE ROGUE MISSILE BLASTS OFF.
THE ROCKET'S MOMENTUM IS ENORMOUS.
STILL, THE WARHEAD ITSELF IS HOUSED IN THE SNOUT.
DON'T NEED TO DEFLECT THE ENTIRE THING.
HOPE THIS WORKS.

SLOWLY, I AWAKEN...
... BOUND.
THE CRUELEST FATE TO WHICH AN AMAZON CAN BE SUBJECTED.
MY BATTERED LIMBS ACHE UNDER THE WEIGHT OF INCARCERATION.
DIVINE MOTHER, GIVE ME STRENGTH.
WELL, WELL... OUR MYSTERY GUEST HAS REVIVED.
SURELY THERE IS MORE TO YOU THAN MEETS THE EYE.
WHILE YOU ARE EXACTLY AS YOU APPEAR, VILLAIN.
YET ANOTHER PETTY, WOULD-BE CONQUEROR WHO HASN'T A CLUE!

OH, YOU'LL FIND THAT I HAVE MORE THAN A CLUE, MY DEAR.
I HAVE AN AGENDA AND A BATTLE PLAN. INDEED, VICTORY ITSELF NOW LIES WITHIN MY GRASP.
MOTHER GAEA HAS SURVIVED FOR EONS WITHOUT YOUR INTERVENTION, VILLAIN.
I SHUDDER TO THINK HOW YOU PROPOSE TO AID HER BY UNLEASHING SUCH WEAPONS OF MASS DESTRUCTION.
THE DIFFERENCE, YOU SEE, IS IN MY PURPOSE.
IN ORDER FOR THE EARTH TO SURVIVE, THEN I MUST NOT FAIL!
A RADICAL CURE, TO BE SURE.
STILL, THE MOST EXTREME CANCERS MUST BE PURGED THUS.
LIFE IS NOT... IS NOT A CANCER.
AH, BUT CIVILIZATION IS.
I SEEK ONLY TO SAVE THE EARTH FROM THE MALIGNANT ACTIONS OF MAN HIMSELF.
MADNESS.
JUST WHO DIED AND MADE YOU SAVIOR, ANYWAY?

HE CAN TELL SHE SUSPECTS AS SOON AS SHE ENTERS THE BARRACKS.
THERE SHOULD BE ARMED GUARDS TO GREET HER.
THE GAS HAS DISSIPATED, BUT AN ODOR STILL LINGERS.
HER FERAL EYES SCAN THE SHADOWS.
HER BODY GOES TAUT, READY TO LASH OUT AT THE SLIGHTEST PROVOCATION.
YOU FORGOT YOUR JACKET.
STILL, HE CAN'T RESIST.

H-YAH!
AGAIN, HER REACTION TIME IS REMARKABLE.
BUT, THIS TIME...
UNPH...
... HE'S READY.
AGGGGH!
WHERE DID ONE SO YOUNG LEARN SUCH MARTIAL SKILLS?
GAIN SUCH INTENSE FEROCITY?

BASTARD! NOBODY TIES ME UP!
GET MY HANDS ON YOU...!
TOK
BE... SORRY...
FSSS
HE HAS NO TIME FOR IDLE SPECULATION.
THE TRACKING SIGNAL LEADS TO AN ABANDONED STORAGE FACILITY.
ONE THAT EXTENDS FAR UNDERGROUND.

I HAD ORIGINALLY PLANNED FOR ONLY TWO MISSILES.
MY FRIEND'S... EXUBERANCE HAS AFFORDED ME A GRAND LUXURY.
I HAVE BROUGHT ONE HERE TO GOTHAM. TO CONFOUND ONE OF MY MOST DOGGED ENEMIES.
FAR BENEATH US RUNS A MAJOR TECTONIC FAULT LINE. DISCHARGED DEEP IN THIS RIFT, THE WARHEAD SHOULD CAUSE A MASSIVE EARTHQUAKE.
ONE THAT WILL DECIMATE THIS CITY THE DETECTIVE SO LOVES.
S-SUPERMAN *WILL* STOP YOU.

THE REMAINING MISSILES WILL BE LAUNCHED INTO THE WORLD'S MOST LUCRATIVE OIL FIELDS. I CAN EVEN SPARE ONE FOR THAT UNFORTUNATE AREA OF THE EARTH KNOWN AS TEXAS.
COUPLED WITH A GLOBAL COMMUNICATIONS BLACKOUT, CHAOS WILL RAGE THROUGH THE CONCRETE JUNGLES OF MAN.
SUPERMAN, YOU SEE, WILL HAVE HIS OWN PROBLEMS TO TACKLE.
MY FORCES STAND READY TO STRIKE IN DOZENS OF MANNERS AND PLACES.
WREAKING HAVOC THAT WOULD KEEP EVEN THE FASTEST DO-GOODER QUITE BUSY.
AND, YOU, MY DEAR... OH, I HAVE SUCH PLANS FOR YOU.
I KNOW FROM PERSONAL EXPERIENCE THE AFTER-EFFECTS OF THE LAZARUS PIT.
THE RESURRECTED TEND TO BE, AT FIRST, QUITE FRISKY. AND THEN, ULTIMATELY, OPEN TO SUGGESTION.
HE PLANS THE DEATH OF MILLIONS ALONG-SIDE MY RAPE, SMILING ALL THE WHILE.
AS IF ARES HIMSELF HAD BIRTHED A HUMAN SON.

ENTERING THE TARGET AREA,
MUST BE CAREFUL TO CONTAIN THE MISSILE NOSE IN ONE PIECE.
TO HAVE IT BREAK APART NOW WOULD BRING DISASTER.

FINALLY...

... PAST THE BLAST RADIUS.

INERTIA THREATENS TO DRAG ME IN.

EVEN IN THIS VACUUM, A RESIDUAL SOUND REACHES MY SENSITIVE EARS.

ONE DOWN, THREE TO GO.
HOPE BRUCE HAS LOCATED THIS MANIAC.

AND NOW, FRIEND, IF I MIGHT BEG ANOTHER FAVOR OF YOU.
PLEASE... CRUSH THE WONDER WOMAN'S SKULL.
WHAT'S THIS? GONE SENTIMENTAL?
OR HAVE YOU FORGOTTEN THE GREAT WRONG SHE HAS COMMITTED UPON YOU?
BIZARRO NOT LIKE GOLDEN ROPE.
DIVINE MOTHER, GRANT ME PEACE...
NOT TODAY, UGLY!

AN EXPLOSIVE BURST FROM A SOLAR-SPECTRUM LASER,
RIGHT BETWEEN THE EYES.
RR-RAAAGH!
SEE, I KNOW YOUR SECRET, CHISEL-FACE.

I'VE READ YOUR FILE!
N-NOOOO!
WHAT WRONG?! BIZARRO EYES...!
BIZARRO NOT SEEEE!
WH-WHAT WAS THAT--?
OVERLOADED ON SUCH AN ENERGY SURGE, THE CREATURE'S PUPILS HARDEN LIKE GEMS.
KRASH!
WHERE IS IT, RA'S?!
WHERE'S THE MISSILE?!
YOU ARE... TOO LATE, DETECTIVE.
NO GAMES, RA'S! WHERE'S THE--

WAK
GHHH--
NNMMMN...?
I'M FINE, UBU.
QUICKLY, WE MUST BE AWAY!
MEET ME AT THE HELIPAD, KILL THE WOMAN IF YOU LIKE, BUT LEAVE THE DETECTIVE ALIVE.
BRAK!
"I WOULD HAVE HIM TASTE HIS DEFEAT!"
PING
CHANK

ARE YOU INJURED?
ONLY MY PRIDE.
SHOULD'VE REMEMBERED THE BODYGUARD WOULD BE CLOSE BY.
YOU...?
NOT GOOD. I TOOK QUITE A POUNDING. SEVERAL OF MY RIBS ARE CRACKED, AND...
...I-- I CAN'T QUITE GET MY VISION FOCUSED.
THAT CREATURE'S POWER IS PHENOMENAL.
FOR YOUR OWN SAFETY, GET OUT OF HERE, IN CASE IT RETURNS.
N-NO! THE MISSILE IS BURIED SOMEWHERE BENEATH US!
HE-- HE INTENDS TO CAUSE A SEISMIC UPHEAVAL.
NOT IF I FIND IT FIRST.
THEN I-- I'M GOING WITH YOU. I'LL BE FINE...
SUIT YOURSELF.
SO LONG AS YOU KEEP UP THE PACE.
AND STAY OUT OF MY WAY.

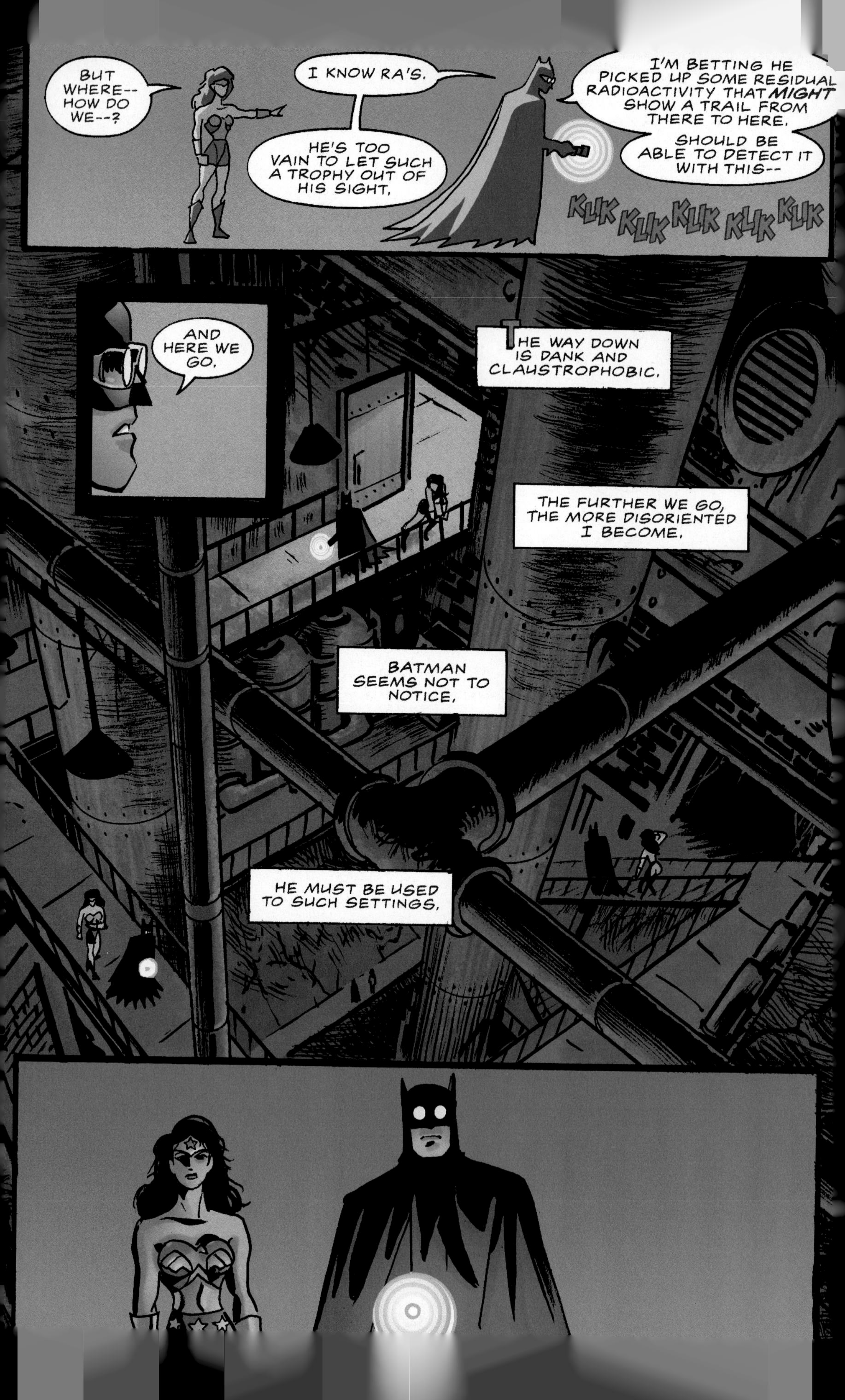
BUT WHERE-- HOW DO WE--?
I KNOW RA'S.
HE'S TOO VAIN TO LET SUCH A TROPHY OUT OF HIS SIGHT.
I'M BETTING HE PICKED UP SOME RESIDUAL RADIOACTIVITY THAT MIGHT SHOW A TRAIL FROM THERE TO HERE.
SHOULD BE ABLE TO DETECT IT WITH THIS--
KLIK KLIK KLIK KLIK KLIK
AND HERE WE GO.
THE WAY DOWN IS DANK AND CLAUSTROPHOBIC.
THE FURTHER WE GO, THE MORE DISORIENTED I BECOME.
BATMAN SEEMS NOT TO NOTICE.
HE MUST BE USED TO SUCH SETTINGS.

NO, WAIT-- THE INSCRIPTION.
WH-WHAT DOES IT--?
NO VISIBLE MECHANISMS. STAND BACK.
I'VE GOT PLASTIQUE IN MY BELT.
IT'S ANCIENT PHOENICIAN.
IT SAYS...
"...FROM THE WELL OF SOULS...
"...RISE THE IMMORTAL DEMON. HIS WILL BE DONE."
GLAD TO SEE YOU PAID ATTENTION IN SCHOOL.
HEY! A WORD OF THANKS MIGHT BE NICE.
YOU'D STILL BE BACK THERE PACKING EXPLOSIVES.
HE IS SO...
YOU KNEW THE SECRET PASSWORD, ACTUALLY. THAT'S SUSPICIOUS.
WHAT?! WHY, YOU--
UNHH... WHAT'S...
...INFURIATING!

WONDER WOMAN!
THOSE... FUMES...
DON'T BREATHE... FUMESS...
FEAR NOT, DEMON HUNTER!
THE VAPORS OF LIFE BEAR YOU NO HARM.
BUT SHE WAS BIRTHED FROM THE SAME MYSTIC MUCK AND MIRE. ITS ESSENCE OVERWHELMS HER.
A LAZARUS PIT.
AND BEYOND IT...

PRECIOUS SECONDS TICK OFF IN HIS HEAD.
YOU ARE TOO LATE TO HALT THE INEVITABLE!
ACCEPT THE DEMON'S WILL IN THIS AS IN ALL THINGS!
THE INERT ROCKET'S CASING ECHOES WITH HIS EVERY STEP.
POP
POP
POP
POP

KNOW THE GLORY OF HIS HOLY CRUSADE!
THE BLAST WILL SEAL HIS RIGHTEOUS CAUSE!
THE CRONE'S STAFF...
...TIPPED WITH A HARDENED SHARD OF THE PIT'S VISCOUS BREW.
ACCEPT THE DEMON'S WILL!
IN THIS AS IN ALL THINGS...
N-N-N...
...HIS WILL BE DONE!
...NEVER, HAG!
NOT WHILE THERE'S A BREATH LEFT TO FIGHT WITH...
SACRILEGE! HERESY!

SNAP!
FEEL THE STING OF HIS MIGHTY WRATH, HERETIC!
AAAHH!
THE PAIN IS SHARP.
AND COLD.
MY TORTURED RIBS SPLINTER AND SHIFT.
MY BLOOD...
... SO MUCH REDDER THAN I REMEMBERED.
WONDER WOMAN!!!

NO TIME...

GGACK!

IN THIS, AS IN ALL THINGS...

HIS WILL BE DOOOOONE--

DON'T TRY TO MOVE!

I'M COMING!
THE WARHEAD'S TIMER ANGRILY CLICKS AWAY.
SECONDS REMAIN.
AN ELECTRO-MAGNETIC PULSE DISRUPTOR.
KLIK
PLANTED DEEP IN THE BOMB'S MECHANICAL GUTS.

HE WONDERS WHETHER THE DEVICE WILL DO ITS WORK.
HE HAS LONG SINCE FORGOTTEN HOW TO PRAY.

THE FALL WAS AWKWARD, YET HE STRUGGLES TO HIS FEET.
MUST HELP...
AS MY LIFE'S BLOOD TRICKLES FROM ME...
...SOME PRIMORDIAL INSTINCT DRAWS ME ONWARD.
MY ONLY HOPE...
...INTO THE PIT.

THE PIT ROILS AS IT UNLEASHES ITS MAGIC.
BASH!
IS IT... THE MONSTER?
NOT HERE!
NOT NOW!
BRUCE, WHAT'S HAPPENED?
SHE WAS GRIEVOUSLY WOUNDED.
SHE... THREW HERSELF INTO THAT ENERGY POOL...
...THE SOURCE OF RA'S AL GHUL'S LONGEVITY.
I-- I CAN'T SEE HER! WHAT'S--
I'VE NEVER WITNESSED THE ACTUAL PROCESS! ONLY ITS AFTER-MATH...

ITS ESSENCE EXPENDED, THE PIT'S OOZE CLINGS TO ME LIKE A BIRTH CAUL.
MY SKIN FEELS LIKE IT'S BEEN SLUICED AND REFITTED.
THE BLOOD IN MY VEINS HAS BEEN RECHARGED.
WITH THE SAME SPARK THAT FIRST GRANTED ME LIFE.

I HAVE BEEN PURGED!
WH-WHAT HAS HAPPENED TO ME?!
WH-- WHAT IS IT?
WHY ARE YOU LOOKING AT ME LIKE THAT?!
Y-YOU'RE FINE, IT'S JUST--
STOP STARING AT ME!!! BOTH OF YOU!
IT'S ALL SO... VIBRANT! SO BRIGHT...
CALM DOWN, YOU'RE IN SHOCK. YOU NEED TO--
YOU DON'T KNOW WHAT I NEED!!!

NO! WAIT!
DIANA... WAIT! I KNOW HOW YOU MUST FEEL...
PLEASE, LET US HELP YOU...
HELP ME?!
YOU KNOW NOTHING ABOUT ME! NOR MY FEELINGS!
DON'T KNOW IF... IF I EVEN KNOW, BUT--
THIS IS WHAT COMES FROM THE WICKED WAYS OF THE PATRIARCH'S WORLD!

DIANA, NO...
DON'T GO...
DIANA?
YEAH. HER NAME IS DIANA.

PARADISE.

ISLAND REFUGE OF THE AMAZONS.
HANG ON...
...YOU SHOULD BE ABLE TO SEE IT PRETTY SOON, NOW.
MYSTICALLY HIDDEN FROM THE PRYING EYES OF THE MODERN WORLD.
BRUCE NEVER LIKES TO FLY WITH ME.
HE INSISTED ON WEARING THE HARNESS. "JUST IN CASE."
THERE.
CHAK!
HE DOES LOVE HIS LITTLE SURPRISES.

WITHIN SIGHT OF THE LANDMASS, HE CUTS FREE.
LIKE I COULDN'T SEE THAT HIDDEN RELEASE MECHANISM.
ON HIS OWN RECONNAISSANCE, HE COMES IN LOW.

LET KENT DRAW ALL THE ATTENTION.

IMMEDIATELY, HE PICKS UP THE SIGNAL.
IRREGULAR, BUT NEARBY.
AN EASY TRACK, BUT STILL...
HE HAS SEEN ALL MANNER OF SETTINGS, YET SOMETHING HERE...
...UNSETTLES HIM.
FOR ONCE, THE COSTUME FEELS HEAVY AND OBTRUSIVE.
IT ITCHES.
HE FINDS HIMSELF DISTRACTED.
BY THE DAPPLE...
...OF SUNLIGHT,
THE FLUTTER...
...OF BUTTERFLY WINGS.
THE SPARKLE...
...OF DEWDROPS.

I HAVE RETURNED.
TO WELLNESS.
THE ISLAND'S HARMONY HAS SOOTHED ME.
HEALED THE RAW EDGE OF MY SOUL'S REBIRTH.
DIVINE MOTHER, BLESSED ARE YOUR GIFTS.
HER GRACE...
...HER SPLENDOR...
...SO UNLIKE THE FRENZIED AFTERMATH OF THE PIT.
UNAWARE, HE SUCCUMBS...

THANK--
GOD--
YOU'RE--
BATMAN?!
WHAT'RE YOU...
...DOING H--MMPH?!!
...OKAY...
...TO THE ISLAND'S ENCHANTMENT.
OVERCOME...
WHAT HAS COME OVER HIM?
UMPH!
REGARDLESS...
...NO ONE MAN-HANDLES ME!

WHY HAVE YOU COME HERE?!
HOW DID YOU FIND ME?!
TRACKING SIGNAL... SLIPPED A BUG INTO YOUR HAIR...
...WHEN I... FREED YOU FROM THE CHAINS...
YOU... YOU THUG!
BUT THAT DOESN'T ANSWER HOW YOU GOT HERE! HOW DID YOU LOCATE THE ISLAND?
DIANA?
ARE YOU ALL RIGHT?!
ONLY HIS SURVIVOR'S REFLEXES SAVE HIS SKULL FROM BEING CRUSHED.
IT'S... A MAN!
AN INTRUDER?!
ON THEMYSCIRA?!
SACRILEGE!!
WHY IS HE DRESSED LIKE THAT?!
ANSWER ME!
SKREEEEEE
FACED WITH DANGER, HIS MIND CLEARS. BRACING TO DEFEND HIMSELF, HE REALIZES...
... THEY ARE ALL...
... WOMEN.

THE SENTRIES SWARM.
BUT DON'T ATTACK. THEIR CRIES ARE A HERALDING.
NOT AN ALARM.
BLESSED APOLLO!
AGAIN...
UM... HI.
...I THRILL AT THE VERY SIGHT OF HIM.

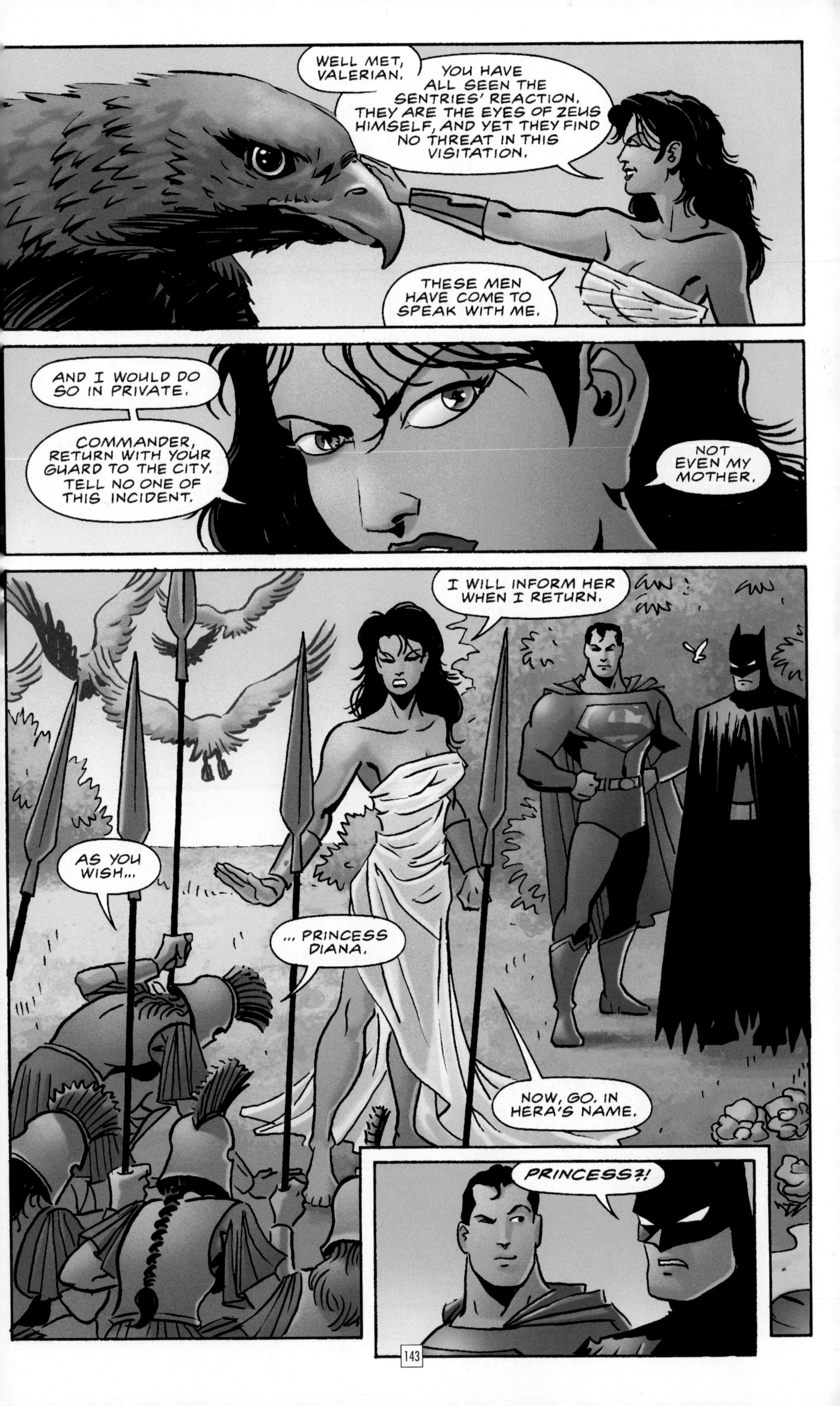
WELL MET, VALERIAN.
YOU HAVE ALL SEEN THE SENTRIES' REACTION. THEY ARE THE EYES OF ZEUS HIMSELF, AND YET THEY FIND NO THREAT IN THIS VISITATION.
THESE MEN HAVE COME TO SPEAK WITH ME.
AND I WOULD DO SO IN PRIVATE.
COMMANDER, RETURN WITH YOUR GUARD TO THE CITY. TELL NO ONE OF THIS INCIDENT.
NOT EVEN MY MOTHER.
I WILL INFORM HER WHEN I RETURN.
AS YOU WISH...
... PRINCESS DIANA.
NOW, GO, IN HERA'S NAME.
PRINCESS?!

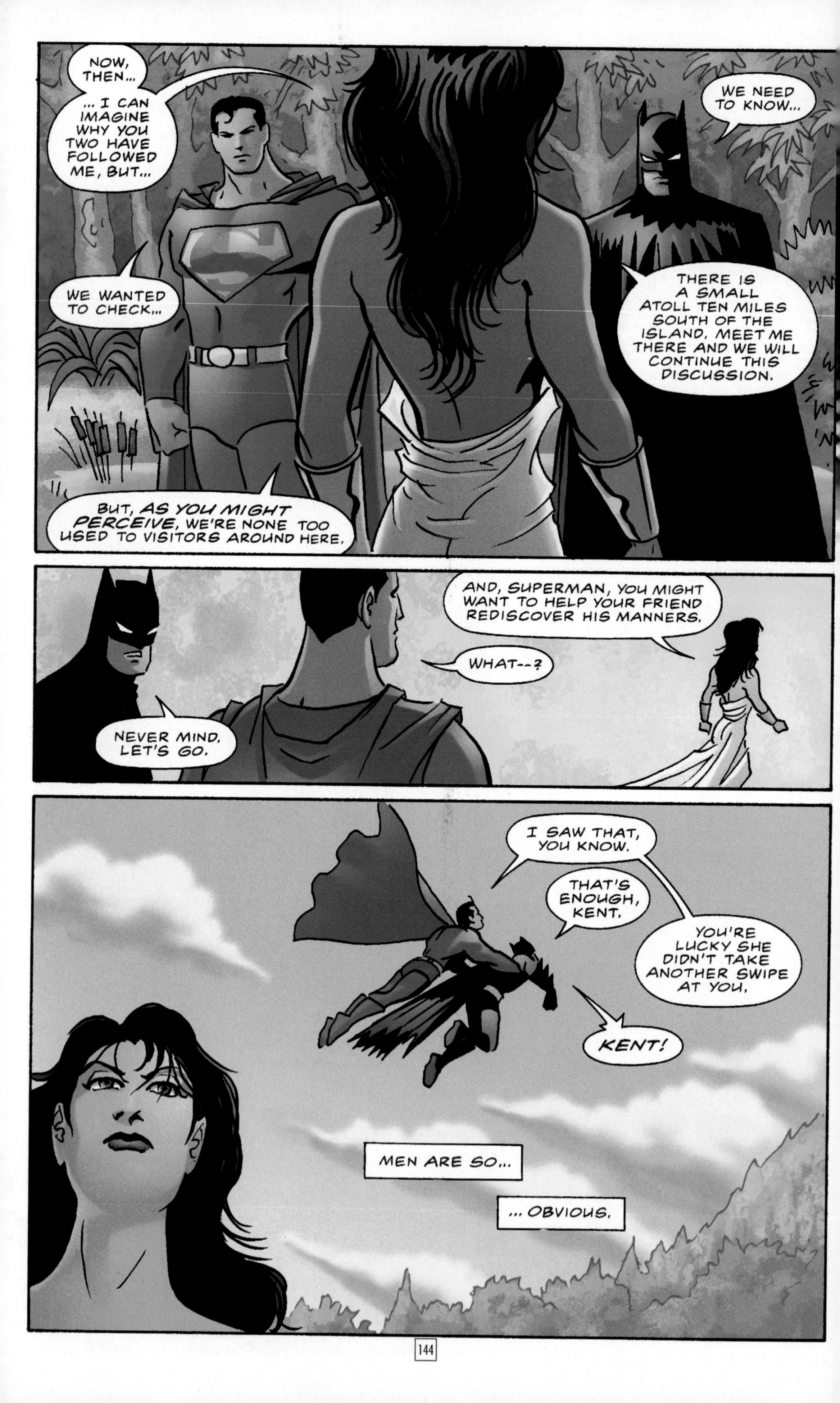
NOW, THEN...
... I CAN IMAGINE WHY YOU TWO HAVE FOLLOWED ME, BUT...
WE NEED TO KNOW...
WE WANTED TO CHECK...
THERE IS A SMALL ATOLL TEN MILES SOUTH OF THE ISLAND. MEET ME THERE AND WE WILL CONTINUE THIS DISCUSSION.
BUT, AS YOU MIGHT PERCEIVE, WE'RE NONE TOO USED TO VISITORS AROUND HERE.
AND, SUPERMAN, YOU MIGHT WANT TO HELP YOUR FRIEND REDISCOVER HIS MANNERS.
WHAT--?
NEVER MIND. LET'S GO.
I SAW THAT, YOU KNOW.
THAT'S ENOUGH, KENT.
YOU'RE LUCKY SHE DIDN'T TAKE ANOTHER SWIPE AT YOU.
KENT!
MEN ARE SO...
... OBVIOUS.

THE GOBI DESERT.
MOST LOGICAL OF THE REMAINING STRONGHOLDS.
WELL HIDDEN.
HEAVILY ARMED.
EASILY DEFENDED.
AT LEAST THAT'S THE THEORY.

SLOW.
SLOPPY.
WHAT KIND OF PROTECTION IS THIS FOR THE WORLD'S MOST WANTED MAN?
TIME TO SHOW THEM HOW IT'S DONE.
ALL OVER AGAIN.

SO...
NO, IT'S FINE. WE UNDERSTAND.
... MY APOLOGIES FOR MY RATHER FRANTIC DEPARTURE FROM GOTHAM.
THE PIT'S MYSTICAL ENERGIES LEFT ME STUNNED AND CONFUSED. I--I'M SORRY FOR ANYTHING I MIGHT HAVE SAID.
RA'S AL GHUL HAS SURVIVED FOR CENTURIES ON SUCH SUPERNATURAL CESSPOOLS.
I CAN IMAGINE ITS EMBRACE IS... OVERWHELMING.
AND I ASSUME THAT THE PURGE IS STILL ACTIVE. THAT'S WHY YOU'VE FOLLOWED ME?
AND CONCERN FOR YOUR WELL-BEING.
I'M JUST GLAD YOU'RE OKAY.
I WANT TO KNOW WHAT AL GHUL REVEALED OF HIS PLANS WHILE YOU WERE HIS CAPTIVE.
AND HOW ONE OF YOUR FELLOW AMAZONS IS APPARENTLY INVOLVED.

I...I DON'T KNOW ABOUT THAT.
HE BRAGGED OF SOME FAR-FETCHED PLAN TO DISRUPT GLOBAL COMMUNICATIONS SYSTEMS.
HE FAILED.
THE MISSILE IN GOTHAM WAS A PERSONAL ATTACK ON YOU, BUT HIS ULTIMATE GOAL WAS TO CONTAMINATE THE WORLD'S MAJOR OIL DEPOSITS.
HE SEEMED TO RELISH THE CHAOS THAT WOULD CAUSE.
HE'S STILL GOT TWO MISSILES.
WHICH MEANS HE'LL HAVE TO CHANGE PLANS.
ARE YOU SURE THERE'S NOTHING ELSE?
NO. MY MEMORY IS FUZZY FROM JUST AFTER THE BIZARRO ATTACKED. AND, LIKE I SAID, THE PIT...
THINK HARDER!
BATMAN, GO EASY.
SHE'S HAD QUITE AN ORDEAL.
WHICH'LL SEEM LIKE NOTHING IF RA'S DETONATES THOSE WARHEADS!
I'M SORRY, BUT THIS IS NO TIME FOR SYMPATHY.
WE MUST FIND RA'S AL GHUL AND DISCOVER WHAT HE NOW PLANS!

ALL THE GREAT CONQUERORS SUFFERED SETBACKS.
GENGHIS KHAN, ALEXANDER, XERXES... ALL LEARNED TO TURN TEMPORARY DEFEATS INTO ULTIMATE VICTORIES. AND NONE OF THOSE BORE SUCH A RIGHTEOUS CAUSE AS THEIR STANDARD.
NOR SUCH A GROUP OF ADVERSARIES ON THEIR TAILS.
THE SATELLITE CONVERGENCE HAS PASSED. AND GOTHAM STILL STANDS, UNSCATHED.
KRRKKK
OH, THAT DAMNED DETECTIVE...
AW, LOOKIT THAT, RA'S, YOUR LITTLE UBU... HE BROKE.
GUESS YOU'LL HAVE TO GET ANOTHER ONE.
HE WASN'T MUCH GOOD WITH HIS JAW BROKEN ANYWAY.
WELCOME BACK, MY DEAR. I KNEW YOU'D RETURN TO US.

IS THAT WHY YOU LEFT ME TO DIE BACK IN GOTHAM?
I HAD NO FEAR FOR YOUR SAFETY, YOUNG ARTEMIS. I KNOW HOW CAPABLE YOU ARE AT TAKING CARE OF YOURSELF.
WELL... UH... GOOD!
WHICH IS MORE THAN I CAN SAY FOR THE SO-CALLED "PURGE"! YOUR TROOP-READINESS IS A JOKE!
I SLIPPED IN HERE WITHOUT A BIT OF TROUBLE.
YES, AND WHO DO YOU THINK LEFT YOUR I.D. SCAN IN THE SECURITY SYSTEM?
BUT, YOU'RE RIGHT.
I DO HAVE NEED OF YOUR MARSHALING OF THE RANKS.
IT IS TIME TO REGROUP AND CONSIDER THE BEST USE OF THE REMAINING ARSENAL.
AND WE MUST BE QUICK ABOUT IT.
EVEN HERE, I HAVE NO DOUBT THE DARK KNIGHT WILL EVENTUALLY FIND ME AGAIN.
NOW YOU'RE TALKIN'! THAT'S ONE OF THE MAIN REASONS I CAME BACK.
'CAUSE WHEN HE DOES, I WANT A CRACK AT HIM!
NOBODY TIES ME UP!

WHAT I NEED IS A SAFE HAVEN. SOMEWHERE UNKNOWN TO BATMAN AND HIS COLLEAGUES.
SOMEWHERE BEYOND REMOTE...
SOMEWHERE...
I... I KNOW A PLACE LIKE THAT. THEY'D NEVER FIND YOU.
IT'S A PERFECT SANCTUARY, BUT YOU WON'T TAKE IT EASILY. BE PREPARED TO FIGHT FOR IT.
FIGHT FOR IT?
MY DEAR, I HAVE SPENT CENTURIES FIGHTING FOR WHAT I BELIEVE.
FOR WHAT THE PLANET NEEDS.
STILL, IT COULDN'T HURT TO ADD A LITTLE MUSCLE FROM OUR "FRIEND" TO THE MIX.
THE CREATURE IS STILL WITH YOU, THEN?
NO, BUT I KNOW WHERE TO LOOK.
AFTER ALL, A WOUNDED BEAST USUALLY RETURNS TO ITS CAGE.

AT THE VERY LEAST, I HAVE A PLAN TO LOCATE THE BIZARRO. EVEN WITH ITS VISION IMPAIRED, THAT MONSTER STILL POSES A TREMENDOUS THREAT.
WHAT DO YOU HAVE IN MIND?
I MANAGED TO TOSS A TRACKING BUG ONTO ITS CAPE JUST BEFORE I CLOCKED HIM.
LIKE THOSE THINGS, DON'T YOU?
I WAS ABOUT TO SLIP ONE ON RA'S WHEN I GOT AMBUSHED.
THE PROBLEM IS, THE DEVICE'S RANGE ISN'T ON A GLOBAL SCALE, AND THAT CREATURE COULD LITERALLY BE ANYWHERE.
I SUGGEST YOU UTILIZE YOUR SUPER-HEARING TO PICK UP THE BUG'S SIGNAL. I'LL GIVE YOU THE FREQUENCY.
IT'S OKAY, I KNOW IT.
BUT, YEAH, THAT SOUNDS LIKE IT COULD WORK.
IT'S A SLIM CHANCE, BUT IT MIGHT PAN OUT.
MEANTIME... ANYTHING YOU COULD DO WOULD BE A BIG HELP, I'M SURE.
NOW JUST A--
I MEAN IT.
HERE.
I SNAGGED THIS BACK IN GOTHAM. I THOUGHT YOU'D WANT IT BACK.
I...
THANK YOU.

I NEED TO RETURN TO THE MAINLAND.
I WANT TO FOLLOW UP A LEAD ON RA'S' WHERE-ABOUTS.
SUPERMAN, YOU KNOW HOW TO FIND ME.
HE DOES LOVE HIS LITTLE SURPRISES.
GOOD LUCK.
LIKE I COULDN'T SEE THE SUB FOLLOWING US.
LUCK'S GOT NOTHING TO DO WITH IT.
WHY?
WHAT?

WHY DO YOU ALLOW HIM TO CONTINUE LIKE THIS?
DON'T HIS METHODS MAKE HIM LITTLE BETTER THAN THE VERY CRIMINALS HE PURSUES?
I KNOW. I FELT THAT WAY ONCE.
MAYBE IT'S THE FACT THAT WE'RE BOTH ORPHANS. I HAD THE BENEFIT OF A FOSTER FAMILY, BUT BATMAN HAD TO GROW UP ON HIS OWN.
BUT MORE IMPORTANT... I KNOW HIS COURAGE.
I'VE SEEN HIM THROW HIMSELF IN HARM'S WAY TIME AND TIME AGAIN, ALL TO RESCUE THE LIVES OF INNOCENTS.
AND, REMEMBER, HE'S GOT NO EXTRAPHYSICAL PROWESS LIKE YOU AND I.
I CAN'T FIND IT IN MYSELF TO DENY THE EXERCISE OF SUCH BRAVERY.
EVEN IF I DON'T ALWAYS AGREE WITH HIS STYLE.
IN FACT, I OFTEN WONDER, IF I WERE AN ORDINARY MAN, WOULD I SHOW THE SAME VALOR?
I'LL BE IN TOUCH.
THE GODS BE WITH YOU.
THANKS.

MEN ARE...
... MORE COMPLICATED THAN I THOUGHT.
FAR BELOW...
... HIS MIND RACES AHEAD OF THE CRAFT.
SCHEMING TO OUTWIT HIS OPPONENT.
SUDDENLY...
... THE SUB...
... TOSSED ABOUT BY...
... DOLPHINS?!
WHY...?
NEARLY CAPSIZED.
HIS FINGER TIGHTENS ON THE FIRING BUTTON.

THEN, JUST AS SUDDENLY...
... THEY'RE GONE.
WHERE...?
YAAA!
TOO FAR.
TOO DEEP.
NO GEAR.
HOW IS THAT...
... POSSIBLE?

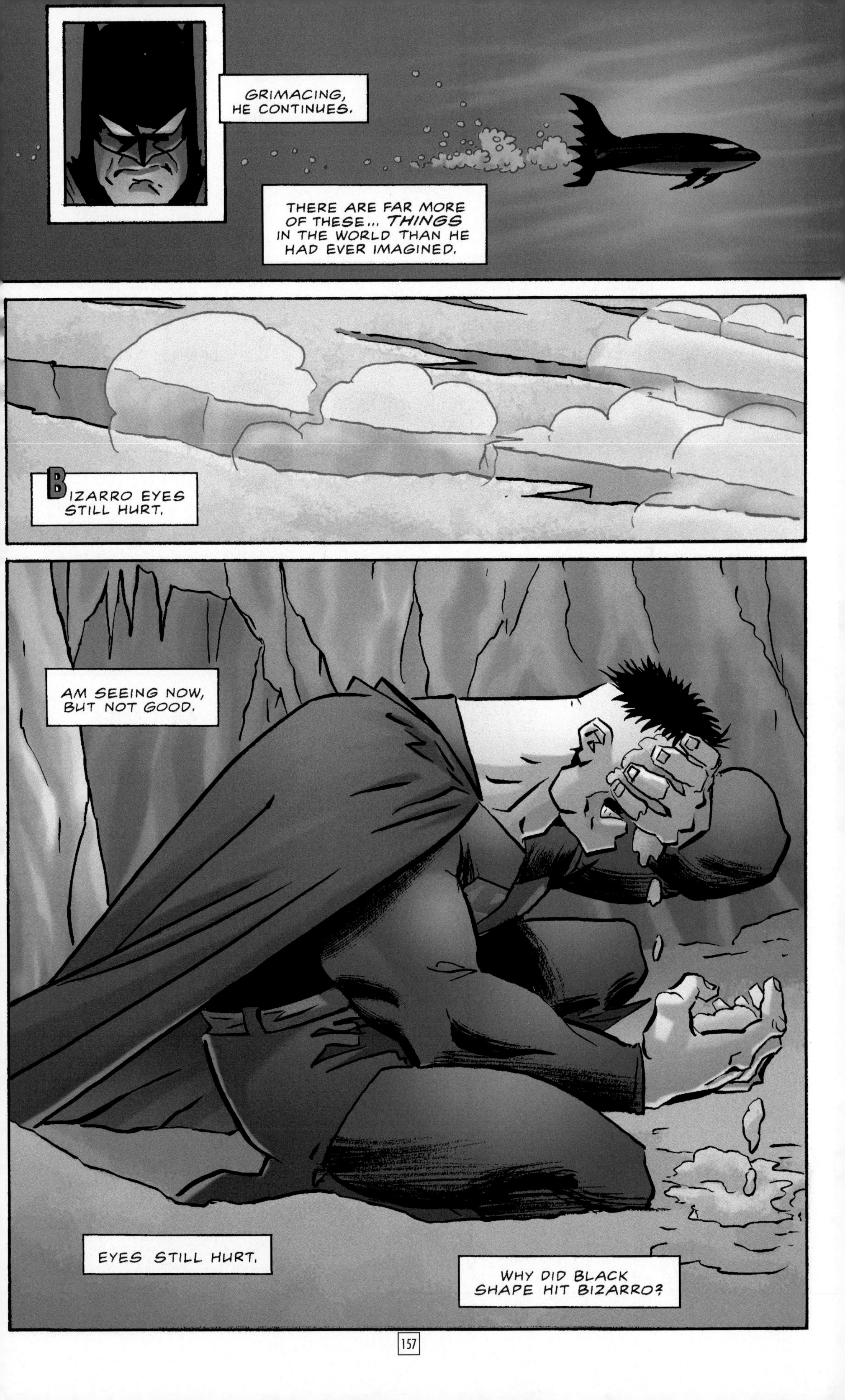
GRIMACING, HE CONTINUES.
THERE ARE FAR MORE OF THESE... THINGS IN THE WORLD THAN HE HAD EVER IMAGINED.
BIZARRO EYES STILL HURT.
AM SEEING NOW, BUT NOT GOOD.
EYES STILL HURT.
WHY DID BLACK SHAPE HIT BIZARRO?

GO 'WAY!
BIZARRO NOT HEAR GOOD, NEITHER.
BUZZING IN HEAD...
UNH--?
...WON'T GO AWAY.
BIZARRO WANT TO BE ALONE.
CALMLY, MY FRIEND...
BUZZING...
I KNOW YOU'VE SUFFERED GREATLY AT THE HANDS OF OUR ENEMIES.
THEY ARE DUE FOR A RECKONING.
...BECOMES VOICE.
BIZARRO KNOW VOICE.
RACER COOL'S VOICE.
TOGETHER, MY FRIEND, WE WILL BRING THEM LOW.
WE WILL MAKE THEM PAY.
BIZARRO #1
RACER COOL AM BIZARRO'S FRIEND.

HIPPOLYTA HAS ALWAYS BEEN A WISE AND JUST QUEEN.
I SEEK HER COUNSEL NOW, AS ALWAYS.
SO, DAUGHTER, HAVE YOU RECOVERED FROM YOUR ORDEAL?
I HAVE, MOTHER, THANK YOU.
YET, SOMETHING STILL TROUBLES YOU?
THE... HEALING BESTOWED UPON ME BY THE PIT. ALTHOUGH RANK BY NATURE, IT STILL FELT SOMEHOW... FAMILIAR.
SUCH MAGIC HAS EXISTED FOR EONS, MY DARLING. ITS POWERS ARE STRANGE TO EVEN THE MOST LEARNED MYSTICS.
I REFER TO THE CIRCUMSTANCES OF MY BIRTH. AM I, TOO, A PART OF SUCH ABERRANT FORCES?
THE WAYS OF THE GODS ARE MANY. BUT YOU ARE A CREATION OF LIFE, NOT A CORRUPTION OF DEATH.
NOW, THEN, AREN'T YOU GOING TO TELL ME ABOUT YOUR... VISITORS?
I SEE RUMOR TRAVELS FAST, DESPITE ANY ROYAL REQUEST.
THEY ARE MY COMPANIONS IN THE PURSUIT OF THIS WORLD-THREATENING EVIL KNOWN AS *THE PURGE.*
ONE OTHER THING TROUBLES ME...
...ONE OF THEM INSISTS THAT ANOTHER AMAZON IS INVOLVED IN THIS WICKEDNESS. HOW CAN THIS BE?

THE WAYS OF THE GODS ARE MANY, INDEED!
WHEN THE AMAZONS WERE GRANTED THE REFUGE OF THEMYSCIRA, A SPLINTER GROUP REFUSED TO ACCOMPANY US.
THEY EVENTUALLY SETTLED IN EGYPT, SURROUNDED BY THE DESERT, EVEN AS WE ARE BY THE SEA.
KNOWN AS THE BANA-MIGHDALL, THEY HAVE LONG RESENTED OUR FAVORED STATUS AMONG THE GODS.
WE HAVE BEEN SEPARATE ALL THESE YEARS.
AND I WONDER IF ONE OF THEM HAS FALLEN IN WITH THE WOLVES OF THE PATRIARCH'S WORLD.
I FEAR IT MUST BE SO.
NOW GO, RETURN TO YOUR MISSION.
CONTINUE THE FIGHT FOR JUSTICE ALONGSIDE YOUR FRIENDS.
THANK YOU, MOTHER. THE GODS BE WITH YOU.
AND WITH YOU, DEAREST DIANA.
A LOST TRIBE?
THEN IT IS ONE OF OUR OWN I PURSUE.

THIS IS TAKING MUCH TOO LONG.
WHY CAN'T I FIND HIM?
BRUCE'S DEVICES, WHILE LIMITED, STILL PROJECT A MUCH STRONGER SIGNAL THAN THE MONSTER'S HEARTBEAT.
SOMETHING MUST BE INTERFERING WITH THE TRANSMISSION.
LIKE WATER, OR...
... EXTREME COLD.

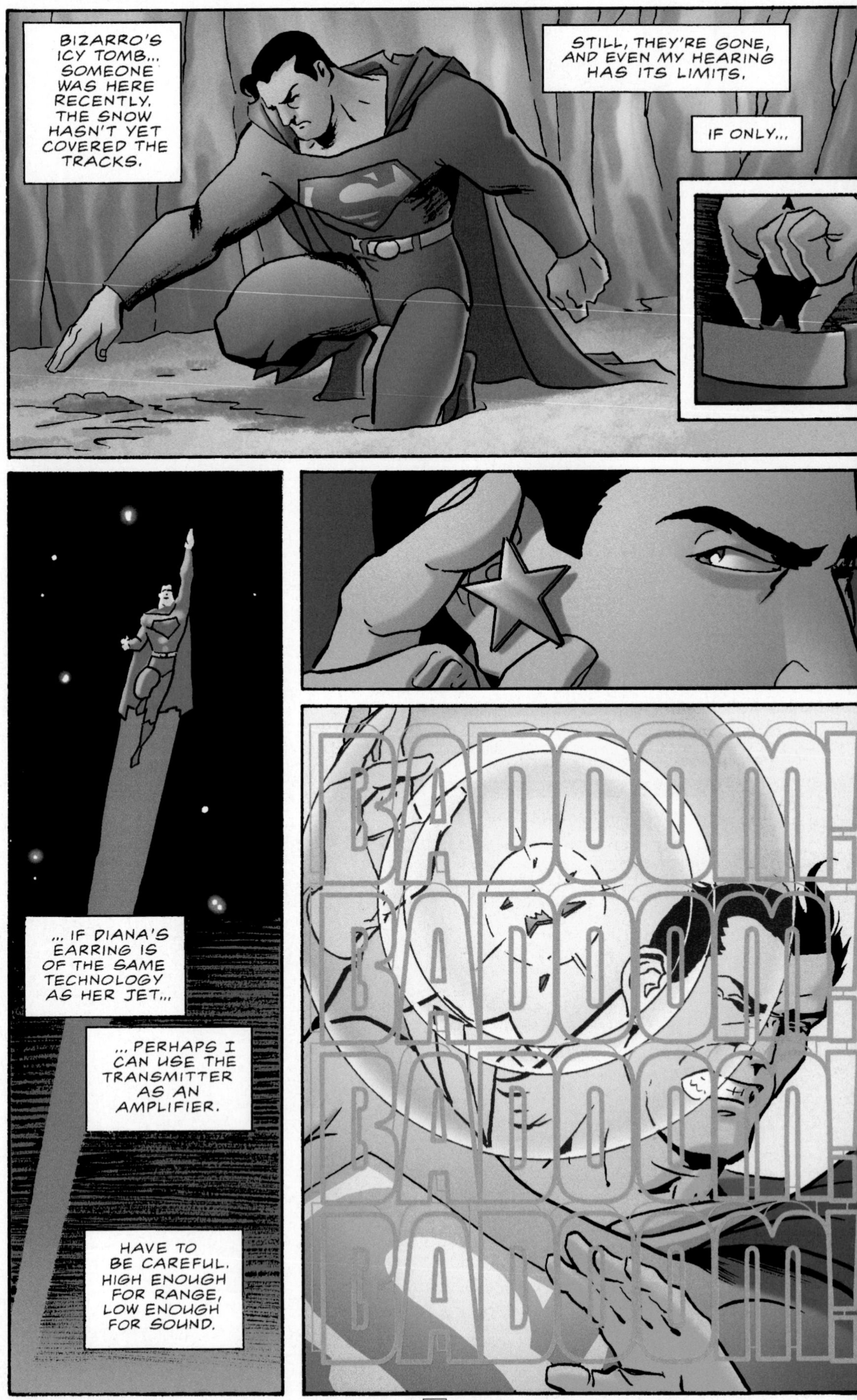
BIZARRO'S ICY TOMB... SOMEONE WAS HERE RECENTLY. THE SNOW HASN'T YET COVERED THE TRACKS.
STILL, THEY'RE GONE, AND EVEN MY HEARING HAS ITS LIMITS.
IF ONLY...
... IF DIANA'S EARRING IS OF THE SAME TECHNOLOGY AS HER JET...
... PERHAPS I CAN USE THE TRANSMITTER AS AN AMPLIFIER.
HAVE TO BE CAREFUL. HIGH ENOUGH FOR RANGE, LOW ENOUGH FOR SOUND.
BADOOM!
BADOOM!
BADOOM!
BADOOM!

ALL RIGHT, YOU BIG, CRAGGY BEAST...
... NOW I'VE GOT YOU.
RA'S HAS THE PATIENCE THAT COMES WITH IMMORTALITY.
HE'S LOST THE BATTLE, BUT NOT THE WAR.
SURELY, HE WILL RETREAT AND REGROUP, HARBORING HIS TERRIBLE WEAPONS AS A SAFETY VALVE.
UM...
ALFRED SAYS WE HAVE A... VISITOR AT THE FRONT DOOR.
YOU GOTTA COME SEE THIS.

AND HOW EXACTLY CAN WE HELP YOU?
MISS...?
THIS IS NO TIME FOR MASQUERADES, MR. WAYNE.
WHEN SUPERMAN VISITED YOU, HE BORE A DEVICE OF MY OWN THAT DOUBLED AS A HOMING BEACON.
MY JET TRACED THE RESIDUAL PATH OF THAT SIGNAL TO A CAVERN LOCATED DEEP BENEATH YOUR MANSION.
TURNABOUT IS FAIR PLAY, AFTER ALL.
W
BUT I'VE COME TO CONFESS THAT YOU WERE RIGHT.
I THINK THERE *IS* AN AMAZON WORKING WITH RA'S AL GHUL.
A RENEGADE.
NOW, IT IS MORE IMPORTANT THAN EVER THAT WE WORK TOGETHER TO OVERCOME THIS THREAT.
AND... I PROMISE I WON'T HIT YOU AGAIN.
GET INSIDE BEFORE SOMEBODY SEES YOU.
ALFRED, ESCORT THE LADY "DOWN-STAIRS."

HOW DO PEOPLE LIVE LIKE THIS? BURIED BENEATH THE EARTH?
HIS OBSESSION RUNS DEEP.
HIS NAME TRANSLATES TO "HEAD OF THE DEMON." HE'S WORTH BILLIONS.
HE'S HAD CENTURIES TO BUILD HIS FORCES AND FORTRESSES ALL OVER THE EARTH.
SO WHERE IS HE NOW?
I'M NOT SURE.
BUT HE'S LIKELY TO GO TO GROUND NOW THAT HIS MAIN OBJECTIVE'S BEEN DERAILED.
AND HE'S STILL GOT THE NUKES.
WHERE'S--?
MASTER BRUCE HAS TAKEN A *FASTER* ROUTE INTO THE CAVERN, MADAM.
WOULD YOU CARE FOR SOME TEA?
NO. THANK YOU.
TWO, TO BE PRECISE.
I THINK HE INTENDS TO USE THEM AS A SAFEGUARD,
TO HOLD HOSTAGE WHEREVER HE PLANS TO HOLE UP.
BUT WHERE?
HE'D HAVE TO MOVE QUICKLY TO ESCAPE DETECTION. HE NEEDS A LOCALE THAT'S ALL BUT UNKNOWN TO THE OUTSIDE WORLD. HE KNOWS I'D EVENTUALLY FIND HIM.
AND, AS YOU SAID...
...HE DOES HAVE AN AMAZON TO SHOW HIM THE WAY.
J

THEMYSCIRA?!! HE'S GOING TO INVADE THEMYSCIRA!!
I NEED TO RADIO AHEAD AND WARN THEM! IF YOU'RE ON BOARD FOR THIS FIGHT, I HAVE A JET THAT'LL GET US THERE QUICKLY!
ABSOLUTELY.
BUT, IF YOU DON'T MIND...
...I'VE GOT SOME GEAR I'D LIKE TO LOAD ON.
A SUPERSONIC JET. TOTALLY INVISIBLE.
HE WANTS ONE.
BIZARRO SEE BETTER NOW, BUT STILL NOT GOOD.
NOT HOT SEE.
NOT FAR SEE.
BIZARRO'S EARS STILL BUZZ.
RACER COOL SAY IT OKAY.

EVEN OVER BUZZ, BIZARRO HEAR...
...SOMETHING FAST--
POW!
PERFECT STRIKE.
CAUGHT UNAWARES, THE MONSTER FLAILS.
AS SEVERAL HUNDRED TONS OF THE MOUNTAINSIDE...

... OBEY THE LAWS OF GRAVITY.
IT'S OVER, GHUL. YOUR INSIDIOUS PLANS ARE THROUGH.
OH, REALLY?
YOU THINK ONE BLOW ENOUGH TO ERADICATE YOUR UNFORTUNATE BROTHER?
HE'S A CLONE. AND I'LL DEAL WITH BIZARRO... AFTER I'VE DISABLED YOUR FLEET.
I SUSPECTED AS MUCH.
THAT'S WHY I'VE LINED UP A SMALL... DISTRACTION FOR YOU.
AT THIS MOMENT, ONE OF MY STRIKE TEAMS IS LAUNCHING A PRECISION ATTACK ON YOUR BELOVED METROPOLIS... ONE THAT WILL SURELY DECIMATE MOST OF THE DOWN-TOWN AREAS.
YOU'RE LYING.
PERHAPS.
STILL, I CAN'T BELIEVE YOUR FABLED SIGHT CAN BEND ITSELF TO SEE HALFWAY AROUND THE GLOBE.
CARE TO TAKE THAT CHANCE?

THIS ISN'T OVER, RA'S!
SIGH
WHY DO THEY ALWAYS INSIST ON SAYING SUCH THINGS?
SUPERMAN HIT BIZARRO!!! BIZARRO TIRED OF BEING HIT!
SUPERMAN AM NOT BIZARRO'S FRIEND!
BIZARRO WILL-- EH?
HE IS GONE, MY FRIEND! BE CALM...
AGAIN, INSIDE BUZZING...
BESIDES, IT'S TIME TO LAUNCH OUR MISSION.
I'LL NEED SOME HELP FROM YOU, CARRYING THE MISSILES.
NOW, COME...
...BIZARRO HEAR RACER COOL.

"... WE HAVE
A KINGDOM
TO CLAIM."
IN THE MANY CENTURIES
SINCE THEIR ARRIVAL HERE...
... THE AMAZONS
HAVE NEVER FACED A
DIRECT INVASION.
NEVER HAD TO FEEL
THE STING OF A MAN'S
BOOT ON THEIR NECKS.
TO THE WOMAN,
THEY WILL DIE IN ORDER
TO DEFEND THE SANCTITY
OF THEIR SHORES.
WHICH, TODAY, JUST
MIGHT BE THE CASE.

THAT MANIAC.
HE WASN'T LYING.
FAR AHEAD, I SEE...
...TWO AIRLINERS, RADIO CONTROLLED BUT LOADED WITH FULL FUEL TANKS.
IF THEY CRASH INTO ANY OF THE SKYSCRAPERS, IT'LL CREATE A MASSIVE CONFLAGRATION.
OF COURSE, THEY GO FOR THE HIGHEST ONE.
JUST WHO SITS AROUND DREAMING UP THIS INSANITY?

I HAD TO LET HIM SLIP THROUGH MY FINGERS TO COME HOME AND SAVE LUTHOR'S DOMAIN.
THE BITTER IRONY DRIVES ME ONWARD.
THE PLANE'S MOMENTUM IS ENORMOUS.
...BUT ITS WING STRUCTURE MAKES ITS VECTOR UNSTABLE, BUT STEERABLE.
HAVE TO TIME THIS JUST RIGHT.

CRASH!
HOPE THIS WORKS.
PERILOUSLY CLOSE...
... THE WOUNDED BIRDS PLUNGE INTO THE LAKE WATERS.
BOOM
LOUD.
BUT HARMLESS.
SOME OF THE WATERFRONT BUILDINGS MIGHT BE FLOODED.
BUT IT BEATS THE ALTERNATIVE.
I'M COMING FOR YOU, GHUL.

AS THE HELLISH FORCES NEAR PARADISE...
... THEIR LEADER ALLOWS HIMSELF A SMILE. FOR THIS, AT LAST, IS BATTLE.
THE DECISIVE DIN HE HAS FED UPON FOR CENTURIES.
SUDDENLY...
... A WATER TROUGH CUTS ACROSS THE POINT-VEHICLE'S PATH,

HOLD UP, FRIEND!
SLOW DOWN! I NEED YOU!
THREATENING TO CAPSIZE...
... AND RUIN EVERYTHING.
SQUAD LEADER?
THEY'RE... THEY'RE FINE! KEEP GOING!
THE MONSTER PAUSES... RIGHT ON TARGET.

A SONIC CONCUSSION DEVICE.
SOMETHING TO THROW HIM OFF BALANCE.
FWUOMM
FOR STARTERS...
YOU TAKE CARE OF RA'S AND THE MISSILES.
I'LL HANDLE BIZARRO.
DONE!
IT... IT'S HER!

TITANIUM MESH.
MEGA-VOLTAGE.
SOMETHING TO WEAKEN HIM.
RRAAGH!
SALT WATER SHOULD SUPER-AMP THE CHARGE.
STINGER GRENADES.
SOMETHING TO CONFUSE HIM.

ONCE AGAIN...
IT'S OVER, GHUL!
YOU WILL NEVER TAKE THEMYSCIRA!
...MY BLOOD BOILS AT THE VERY SIGHT OF HIM.
ON THE CONTRARY! ITS PURITY IS EXACTLY WHAT I SEEK!
WHAT'S MORE, IT LIES HIDDEN FROM ANY DETECTION. THAT, COUPLED WITH MY BRACE OF DETERRENTS, MAKE IT THE PERFECT SAFE HAVEN.
BESIDES, WHEN I SOMEDAY ACHIEVE MY GOALS...
...THE CURRENT POPULACE WILL MAKE A HEARTY BREEDING STOCK...
KANG
...TO RE-POPULATE THE NEW WORLD!
AS IF ARES HIM-SELF HAD BIRTHED A MORTAL SON.

LIKE A DERVISH, HIS ATTACKS RAIN ON MY SHIELD.
IS HE DRUGGED?
INCOMING...
HIGH ABOVE, THE SENTRIES OF ZEUS LEAD THE FIRST WAVE OF DEFENSE.
BUT EVEN ENCHANTED EAGLES...
BADDA BRAKKA BAKKA BRADDA BRADDA BAKKA
...ARE NO MATCH FOR A HIGH-CALIBER SALVO.

TIME FOR THE CLOSE-UP STUFF.
MOUNTED SOLAR LASERS.
RELEASE A BLAST WITH EVERY PUNCH.
MUSCLE AND FLESH HARDEN AND CRACK.
TRY TO TAKE OFF A CHUNK OF HIS FACE.
AS ALWAYS, IT'S THE SPEED THAT SO AMAZES.
SPEEDING BULLETS...

UNIT TWO, CAREFUL!
THE BLOOD OF AMAZONS.
SO MUCH REDDER THAN SHE IMAGINED.
SHE CANNOT DO THIS.
OUT!
SHE CANNOT CAUSE THE DEATH OF HER OWN.
WHAT WAS SHE THINKING?

CHANK
HA! REGARDLESS OF ALL YOUR "WONDERS"...
YOU ARE STILL JUST A WOMAN!
AND I DON'T NEED ANY EXTRAS...
...TO COMBAT THE LIKES OF YOU!
HIS EYES ARE GLAZED WITH BATTLE LUST.
AMAZINGLY, HIS ATTACKS DESCEND EVEN FASTER.
THE AIR RINGS WITH OUR CLASHING.
FINALLY...
...ONE CUT SLIDES THROUGH.

SNAP!
YOU HAVE DRAWN FIRST BLOOD, GHUL!
BUT I WILL END THIS CONFLICT!
LEADERLESS, THE FLIGHT SQUADRON DOESN'T REALIZE THEY ARE UNDER ATTACK...
... FROM WITHIN THEIR OWN RANKS.
AIRCRAFT STRIKE THE WATER. BUT SOME...
... MANY, NOT IN FLAMES, AND...
... WITHOUT THEIR PROPELLERS?

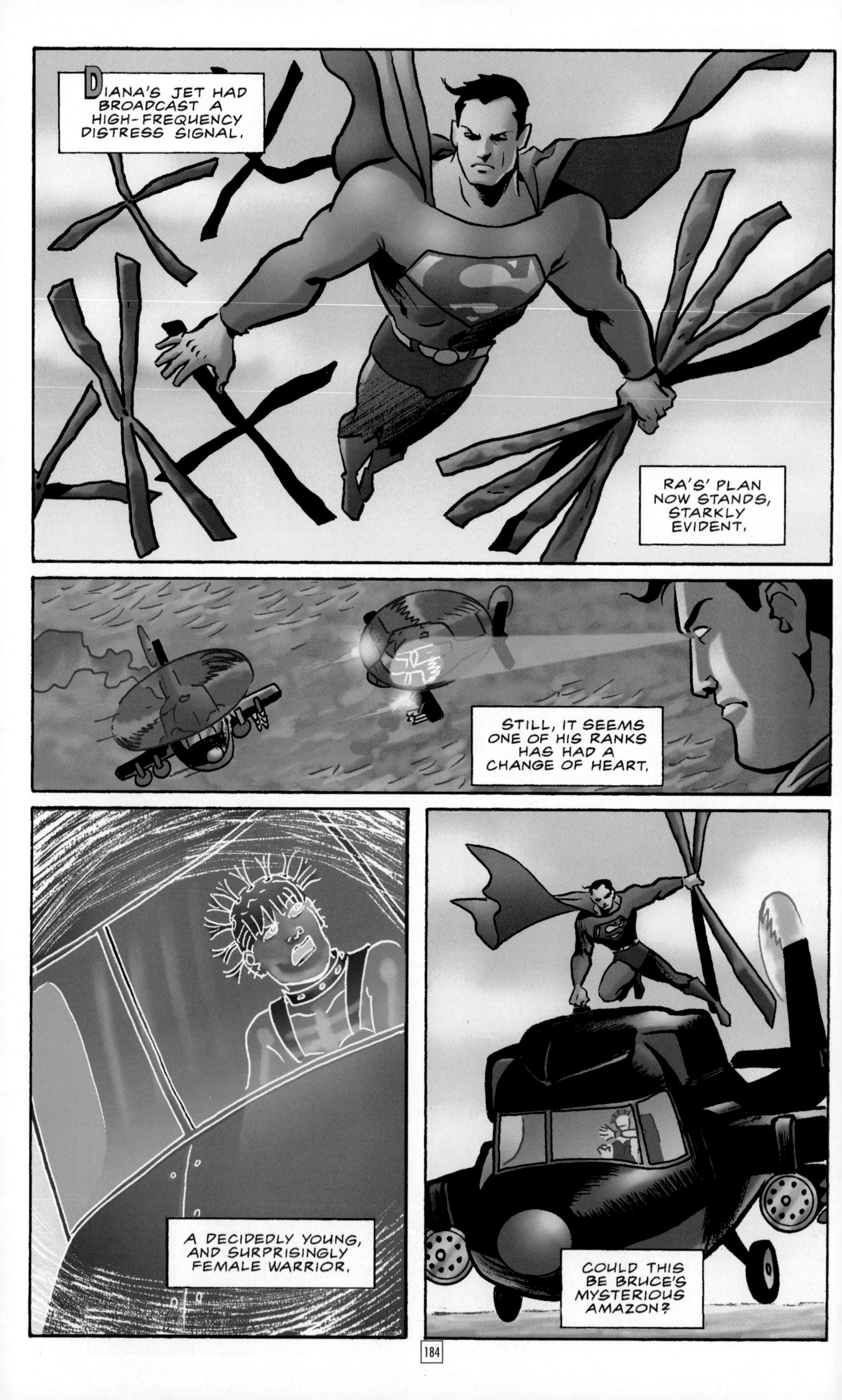
DIANA'S JET HAD BROADCAST A HIGH-FREQUENCY DISTRESS SIGNAL.
RA'S' PLAN NOW STANDS, STARKLY EVIDENT.
STILL, IT SEEMS ONE OF HIS RANKS HAS HAD A CHANGE OF HEART.
A DECIDEDLY YOUNG, AND SURPRISINGLY FEMALE WARRIOR.
COULD THIS BE BRUCE'S MYSTERIOUS AMAZON?

YOUR CAUSE IS HOPELESS, WOMAN!
YIELD NOW AND I WILL MAKE YOU MY FAVORED CONSORT!
CONTINUE, AND YOU WILL SURELY PERISH!
ENOUGH!
I'VE HAD ENOUGH OF YOUR CALLOUS ARROGANCE!
YOUR ASSUMPTIONS OF GRANDEUR AND RIGHTEOUSNESS!
YOU ARE NO WORLD SAVIOR, DEMON!
YOU ARE PATHETIC!!!

I SUPPOSE I MUST GO IN AFTER HIM.
THE MONSTER'S TORTURED FACE CRACKLES WITH RAGE.
ITS BREATH SMELLS LIKE A CHEMICAL FURNACE.
ONLY ONE CHANCE TO STAVE OFF ITS ATTACK.
HIT HIM HARD WHERE IT ALREADY HURTS.
UNGH!
RAAAGH!
BIZARRO NO LIKE BLACK SHAPE MAN.

THWAK!
BATMAN--
THE CREATURE--
BLACK SHAPE MAN HIT BIZARRO IN EYES.
AGAIN!
NOW BIZARRO HIT BACK.
IN EYES.
GAAHH!
NOW WHO MIGHT YOU BE?
AND AREN'T YOU A LITTLE YOUNG TO BE PILOTING AN ASSAULT HELICOPTER?
HE SHINES LIKE THE SUN GOD COME TO EARTH.
A-A...
NO!

HIS SCARLET CLOAK, PROUDER THAN ANY SPARTAN'S.
M-MY NAME IS ARTEMIS.
I-I'M ONLY FOURTEEN.
WITH EVERY OUNCE OF MY STRENGTH, I FIGHT TO RESTRAIN...
... THE CREATURE'S RAGE.
SLOWLY...
... I AM...
... LOSING.

AND, SUDDENLY, HE IS THERE.
FROM HIS EYES...
... THE FIRES OF MOUNT VULCAN.
NAAAAAGHH!
SSSSSS

PART OF ME REGRETS THE MONSTER'S PAIN.
EVEN AS THE FARM BOY IN ME RECOGNIZES...
...A MAD BEAST THAT MUST BE PUT DOWN.
BATMAN, ARE YOU ALL RIGHT?
C-CAN'T... B-BREATHE--
ARMOR... C-CRUSHED--
HOLD STILL.
GASP!
CHANK!

I GIVE HIM NO TIME TO RECOVER.
POUNDING HIM SENSELESS.

AND NOW, TIME TO IMPRISON HIM.
SOMEWHERE I SPIED ON THE HURRIED FLIGHT HERE.

THE MINERAL-RICH MAGMA APPEARS AS LITTLE MORE THAN SLUDGE TO MY SPECIAL SIGHT.
DEEP IN THE VOLCANO'S BOWELS...
...I FIND NO TRACE OF THE CREATURE.
PERHAPS THE HARDENING ROCK WILL HOLD HIM AS TIGHTLY AS HIS ARCTIC TOMB.

I SCANNED FOR RA'S' BODY BENEATH THE WAVES.
NO LUCK.
IF HE WAS CAUGHT IN THE GULF STREAM, HIS CORPSE COULD'VE BEEN SWEPT ANYWHERE BY NOW.
POSEIDON'S KINGDOM IS VAST.
LEAVE HIM. AND GOOD RIDDANCE.
WHATEVER'S... DOWN THERE... CAN HAVE HIM.
THERE.
I'VE DISCONNECTED THE FIRING MECHANISMS. THE WARHEADS ARE INERT.
I'M MELTING THE METAL SURROUNDING OF THE CORE INTO A HARDENED LUMP. IT SHOULD KEEP THE PLUTONIUM FROM LEAKING OUT.
IT'S DONE.
TIME TO CONSIGN THESE INSTRUMENTS OF DEATH TO THE DEEP.
POP

IN THE AFTERMATH...
...I CONSIDER HOW CLOSELY WE HAD VEERED TOWARDS UTTER DISASTER.
WITHOUT DIANA'S SENSE OF SACRIFICE AND BRUCE'S UNSHAKABLE REASONING...
...IT MIGHT'VE ALL TURNED OUT SO VERY DIFFERENT.
I AM LUCKY TO COUNT THEM AS FRIENDS.
A SEARCH OF THE SURVIVORS TURNED UP NO TRACE OF THE RENEGADE AMAZON.
I MAY NEVER KNOW WHO IT WAS THAT CAME SO CLOSE TO DESTROYING ALL THAT I HOLD DEAR.

I AM COMFORTED TO KNOW THAT I NOW HAVE TWO COMRADES WHO WOULD DO ANYTHING TO PREVENT THAT.
GOOD THINGS COME IN THREES.

HE HAS NO DOUBT THAT RA'S AL GHUL WILL SOMEDAY SURFACE TO TROUBLE HIM AGAIN.
IT HAS HAPPENED BEFORE.
AND SO, HE CONTINUES THE FIGHT... FOR JUSTICE.
BUT NOW, FOR SOME-THING ELSE, AS WELL.
A MEMORY.
OF SUNLIGHT. AND DEWDROPS.
HE HAS SEEN PARADISE.

EPILOGUE:
THANK YOU, UBU.
I LIVE ONLY TO SERVE YOUR FATHER, MISTRESS.

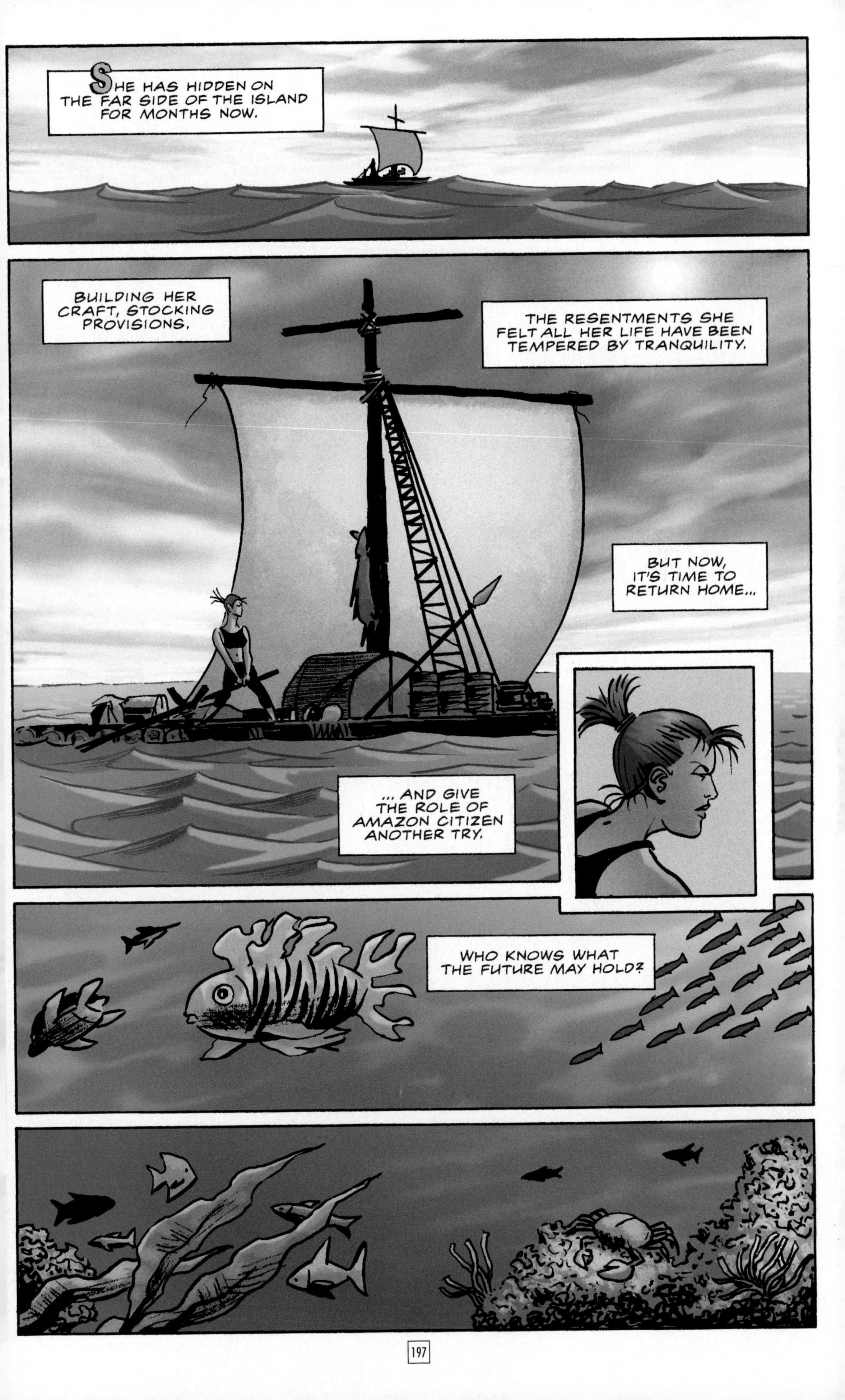
SHE HAS HIDDEN ON THE FAR SIDE OF THE ISLAND FOR MONTHS NOW.
BUILDING HER CRAFT, STOCKING PROVISIONS.
THE RESENTMENTS SHE FELT ALL HER LIFE HAVE BEEN TEMPERED BY TRANQUILITY.
BUT NOW, IT'S TIME TO RETURN HOME...
... AND GIVE THE ROLE OF AMAZON CITIZEN ANOTHER TRY.
WHO KNOWS WHAT THE FUTURE MAY HOLD?

THE END

BATMAN/SUPERMAN/WONDER WOMAN: TRINITY #2 cover

ADVENTURES OF SUPERMAN #628
Trinity-themed cover

WONDER WOMAN #204
Trinity-themed cover

BATMAN #627
Trinity-themed cover

DC
WONDER

-BIZARRO

-ARTEMIS
-RÁS AL GHUL